Night Whispers 'A Kingdom in A State'

Volume 02-Q2

April-May-June

Edition 01-Revision 04

Victor Robert Farrell

I0083075

NightWhispers
All current
Contact & Sales Information
Can be found at
www.NightWhispers.com

Night Whispers
'A Kingdom in A State'
Volume 02–Q2
April-May-June

Copyright © Rev. Victor Robert Farrell

2019

ISBN Number 978-1-910686-10-2

First published in this format

February 2016 by WhisperingWord

All current contact and sales information can be found at

www.NightWhispers.com

Printed in The United Kingdom

for

WhisperingWord Ltd.

Night Whispers

'A Kingdom in A State'

Volume 02-Q2

April-May-June

Dedication

This book is dedicated, very simply,

To the now four most important people

In the whole wide world to me.

My daughter Gemma,

My son Jonathan,

My grandaughter Ellie May,

And of course,

My wife

Bridget.

PREFACE

I am Pastor, Rev. Victor Robert Farrell, and these everyday Bible insights called 'NightWhispers' have long since been a global endeavor to communicate the God of the WHOLE Bible in very raw terms to very real people. This is my passion and the reason why I founded The 66 Books Ministry, who, through our 66 Cities project, over the course of the next 25 years, by the grace of God and according to His will and favor, shall be preaching consecutively from each of the 66 Books of the Holy Bible, the Gospel of the Lord Jesus Christ in 16,500 of the most influential cities of the world on an annual and ongoing basis! In this regard, these NightWhispers accompany our endeavors by providing Every Day Insights into the whole Bible.

These NightWhispers are presented in such a way as to be read each day. They are produced on a regular basis, and the 366 daily readings for each year are presented with a unique volume number. That 'Volume' year is then divided into four Quarters. For example:

Year 01= Volume 01-Q1 | January-February-March
Year 01= Volume 01-Q2 | April-May-June
Year 01= Volume 01-Q3 | July-August-September
Year 01= Volume 01-Q4 | October-November-December
Year 02= Volume 02-Q1 | January-February-March
Followed by Volume 3, 4, 5, 6 etc., and the associate four Quarters for the consecutive years. I am sure you get the picture!

The point is, that you can start any volume of NightWhispers IN ANY YEAR you wish, and AT ANY TIME you choose, because whilst these Everyday Bible Insights are fresh and relevant to each day, they are not interconnected in a way, which means you have to read one volume before another. Indeed, NightWhispers are produced as stand-alone products rather than connected volumes. Therefore, if you wish, you can also consecutively read any Quarter from any Volume you choose! For example: Volume 02-Q3 might easily be followed by Volume 05-Q4, because each book is a standalone product. Got it? Excellent! So, now that I have most thoroughly confused you, may I say that along with the team at The 66 Books Ministry and Whispering Word, I do hope and pray that these particular *NightWhispers,* will be an enormous blessing to you in *revealing just a little more to you of the God of the WHOLE BIBLE.*

Rev. Victor Robert Farrell, June 2019, Scotland

INTRODUCTION TO NIGHTWHISPERS

VOL 02-Q2- 'A Kingdom in A State'

This is our sixth standalone quarterly volume of NightWhispers and we hope that these Every Day Bible Insights will be mighty food supplements to arm you for the present spiritual conflict and the coming fight of this dark night.

Spring is here, and remember, that it is the time when Kings go out to war. Look now, the West has rejected the message and the people of the Book, of the Cross, and of the Lamb of God. In rejecting these things it has hardened its heart, corked its ears and blinded its own eyes. It is beyond redemption and no amount of prayerful cajoling by ourselves is going to change that. The legacy church, those churches that are culturally compromised and lukewarm have been a great catalyst in this hardening effect. Therefore, I suspect that if there is to be a turning to the God of the Bible it will be outside of the present church structures, for her Lord is refusing to reform it, but rather, is throwing it out with the refuge. In addition to this, our western nations have rejected the God of the Bible. Currently, the State now presents the true Biblical church with soft persecution. It shall soon turn to hard persecution and the compromised church shall join the state in that persecution! Therefore, it is time to build the 'Kingdom within a State,' and a what a bloody state it is. It is time to for the true people of God to separate from the Laodicean mob, so as not to subjugate ourselves any farther to the false Gospel being pedaled. It is time to rebuild those one separate free standing Gospel structures which kept us somewhat safe. It is time to get ready for the dark night of the soul of this earth, it is time to build a 'Kingdom within a State.' In every way, the local church must take time to take care of its own people. Look now, let us love and take care of one another and build structures that enable this to be so. If we do not do this now, then should a remnant remain in the West, it shall be exceptionally impoverished in every way. Apart from being simply the remains of s spiritual gene pool, it shall be redundant.

As usual, all we earnestly desire is that you especially check the Scriptures to see if these things are so, and also to do your own digging both there in particular and elsewhere in general. May God the Holy Spirit truly guide you in this.

Some global historical acknowledgements

Now then, I have been writing these Bible Insights for many years and I have gleaned in a multitude of fine meadows and otherwise. For me to give credit where credit is due then, would not only increase the size of this quarterly volume many, many times, but I would undoubtedly miss many more people out of that massive list of those which I tried to give credit to. It is Solomon who said that *"there is nothing new under the sun"* and I believe it! Therefore, please then take it for granted that when someone like myself, who almost sees 'cut and paste' as an unspoken gift of the Holy Spirit, says he might have gleaned from another person's work, in someplace, somewhere, and at some point in time without giving appropriate credit where credit is due, that I probably have! If this is the case, it was not my intention to rob you of any glory, but if I have, then please inform me of the same and the necessary changes and/or credits will be made. Remember, I have borrowed from everywhere, I have taken from everyone. 'Everywhere' and 'everyone;' there you go, that should have you covered!

US, UK or elsewhere-or, "How do you spell that?"

To be British, is to be somewhat like 'the last of the Mohicans.' The Britain, that is, the United Kingdom I grew up in is breaking apart. No, sadly, it is broken and never to be repaired. Even so, I am of Irish & Scottish great-grandparents, grandparents and parents, and I was also born in England. Therefore, I am British and a Celt at that. In addition to this, I love North America and the South in particular, so much so, that I feel like a British Red-Neck. Does this make me a Yankophile, or loving the South in particular (and its battle flag) does it make me more especially a Dixiophile? Alternatively, maybe I could be an Americophile or a Canameriphile? Who knows? Suffice to say, that as our nations were once only divided by a common 'English' language, (America still being the residence of the majority of our English readers,) I have tried to adopt the spelling and grammar of the Americas. In this, I have no doubt failed, and in the so doing, both mixed and matched the UK and US spelling and English grammatical styles. In doing this, I confess that I am a double-minded man, and unstable in all my editorial ways. The purists, either side of the pond, I am sure will never forgive me. The rest do not care. Either way, I need your help. So, if you spot any 'howlers,' do let me know. Email me your corrections on,

getyouracttogetherman@whisperingword.com

BIBLE VERSIONS

Ah, the Bible. The true meta-narrative of the real world and therefore all things   meta-physical. Well, preferring the 'Textus Receptus' or the 'Majority Text,' I have tried to use the New Separatist Bible (NSB), which is a confluence Bible based on the 1560 Geneva Bible and the 1611 Authorized version, (Pure Cambridge Edition)   when I have referenced the Bible, though where necessary, for mere contemporary clarity of course, when I have I have deviated from this norm, at that time I have clearly indicated which other Bible Version has been referenced.

NIGHTWHISPERS ARE WRITTEN FOR........

There is so much 'devotional' material available nowadays for the Christian that a great part of me says that no more should be written. Yet I do believe that we are moving speedily to the time of the end. What devotionals are written to truly address the needs of Christians living in the approach to this period, or in this period? In my opinion, there are none. NightWhispers then, are written for those people of this darkening time in particular. Therefore, you will find that NightWhispers are battle rations that demand your time, attention, study and consideration. If you need a little ear tickler folks, a quick little cuddle before you go to bed at night, a sleeping pill even, indeed, if you have sold out the truth, your calling and your very self for ten shekels and a shirt, then these Bible Insights are NOT for you. They demand your thoughtful consideration and further investigation and ardent application. They need your time! NightWhispers are written for those seekers who are looking for the God of the whole Bible. They are written for those who hate the color grey but love black and white. They are written for those who want to know the truth, even if it is unpalatable to them. They are written for the awakened; that is, for those people who know that the darkness is alive and like a black incoming tide, is infiltrating every area of present life. They are written for those people who know that a Night is coming when no man can work. They are written for those people who refuse to be spoon-fed. They are written for Bible hungry people. They are written for those who are done with distractions. They are written for those people who have not sold out to cultural compromise and refuse to sell themselves to social niceness and religious self-righteousness. They are written for those who want to cease being unpaid social workers for the unthankful and want to love and arm the saints. They are therefore written for fighters, even that growing band of brothers who are no ragged or rag-tag remnant, but rather, are the released people of 'The Revolution,' that back to the Bible, boots on the ground, present movement of God, who are done with everything that has silenced the one true church and with the removal of its voice, have killed our nations. They are written for the sold out the followers of Christ who have at last found their proclamation voice. They are written for the rooted, fruited and flowering stump. Therefore, to all you great and holy people then, who, even in this darkness might just turn the world right ways up once more, I say then this to you this very night:
"Welcome to NightWhispers, Volume 02-Q2- 'A Kingdom in A State.'
"Be strong and keep looking up for your salvation draweth nigh."

JUST A HUCKSTER

Some young preacher will study until he has to get thick glasses to take care of his failing eyesight because he has an idea he wants to become a famous preacher. HE'S JUST A HUCKSTER buying selling and getting gain. They will ordain him and he will be known as Reverend and if he writes a book, they will make him a doctor. And he will be known as Doctor; but he's still a huckster buying and selling and getting gain.

***And when the Lord comes back,
HE will drive him out of the temple
along with the other cattle.***

A.W. Tozer

(from 'Tozer on Christian Leadership,' compiled by Ron Eggert)

John 3:30 He must increase
but I must decrease.

STILL LOOKING

Wise men speak of trees
From the Cedar to the Hyssop
Springing from the wall
From the Aspen to the Alder
Beside the water fall

Wise men speak of animals of creeping things and fish
Of birds and bees and smooth black cats
That lap the dainty dish

Wise men sing of love and capture moments in a jar
Wise men suck the juice of days
Wise men shop at Spar!

Wise men count the fallen ticks
Of old clocks running down
Wise men number muscles
That help create the frown

Wise men follow after
Wise men follow far
Wise men seek the Savior still
Beneath the wandering star

1 Kings 4:33 Also he spoke of trees, from the cedar tree of Lebanon even to the hyssop that springs out of the wall; he spoke also of animals, of birds, of creeping things, and of fish. (NKJV)

The Old 100th!

All people that on earth do dwell,
Sing to the Lord with cheerful voice.
Him serve with fear, His praise forth tell;
Come ye before Him and rejoice.

The Lord, ye know, is God indeed;
Without our aid He did us make;
We are His folk, He doth us feed,
And for His sheep He doth us take.

O enter then His gates with praise;
Approach with joy His courts unto;
Praise, laud, and bless His name always,
For it is seemly so to do.

For why? the Lord our God is good;
His mercy is for ever sure;
His truth at all times firmly stood,
And shall from age to age endure.

To Father, Son and Holy Ghost,
The God whom Heaven and earth adore,
From men and from the angel host
Be praise and glory evermore.

From 'Fourscore and Seven Psalms of David'
(Geneva, Switzerland: 1561); attributed to William Kethe

CONTENTS

| Vol 02 | Q2 | NW00458 | April 01st |

'Mocking Death' or, 'Dancing on your own casket!'

One critic has accused the metaphysical poet John Donne (he died March 31st in 1631,) of being obsessed with death after his beloved wife Anne passed away. Maybe so, for shortly before his own demise, John obtained an urn, his own burial shroud, and an artist. Then, wrapping himself in the shroud, he posed standing atop that same urn and had the artist draw a nice charcoal sketch of him doing so. This macabre piece of artwork stayed at John's bedside throughout his final illness. Obsessed or not, in his poem, 'Death Be Not Proud,' he pens these marvelous lines,

1 Cor 15:53-58

So when this corruptible has put on incorruption, and this mortal has put on immortality, then shall be brought to pass the saying that is written: "Death is swallowed up in victory."

"O Death, where is your sting?

O Hades, where is your victory?"

The sting of death is sin, and the strength of sin is the law. But thanks be to God, who gives us the victory through our Lord Jesus Christ. Therefore, my beloved brethren, be steadfast, immovable, always abounding in the work of the Lord, knowing that your labor is not in vain in the Lord. NKJV

"Death be not proud,
though some have called thee
Mighty and dreadful,
for thou art not so:
death shallt die."

Now John may have been an Anglican minister simply because it was a reasonable living (in those days anyways,) and he may have held, shall we say, some interesting theological thoughts! But he at the very least knew this great Christian truth, "death shalt die."

Friends, everything this side of heaven dies, that is in effect, becomes severed in relationship to us. Dreams, words, sons, daughters, wives, jobs, careers, teeth, and eventually even the flesh that holds them all together, shall dissolve and disintegrate. We shall be severed from everything and everyone we are currently connected to These are facts, and are best faced, head on.

The Scripture says, *"Better to go to the house of mourning than to go to the house of feasting, for that is the end of all men; and the living will take it to heart." (Ecclesiastes 7:2).* In light of this text then, maybe Rev Donne wasn't as bananas as we might have thought after all?

If you must, go buy a grave plot and picnic upon it, even plant a tree in it! MOCK DEATH CHRISTIAN for death shalt die but you shall live forever!

My dear friend if you are suffering under the fear of death, suffering in the valley of the shadow of death, may I tell you that I agree with John Donne when he says, *"Death be not proud, though some have called thee Mighty and dreadful, for thou art not so: death shalt die."* If you want rest today my friend, I mean truly rest from your fears of death, then you must mock death, go on! Do it! I am not saying throw your life away, I am not saying be unnecessarily daring and put your life at risk! That's stupidity. No, I am saying Mock death. Then laugh at it and choose to lay off it's proud and heavy disfiguring yoke and then, why not place across your chaffed neck, the gentle healing, loving and leading, humble yoke of the all-conquering Christ; for death truly has been swallowed up in victory! Yes it has! So, finish of the delightful deed of mocking death today, by then taking your Palm branches, and standing on one leg atop your own urn of death, and wave them wildly. Why not get one of your friends to then take a picture of you, dancing like a loon atop your murky old casket once filled with gloom! If you must, go buy a grave plot and picnic upon it, even plant a tree in it! MOCK DEATH CHRISTIAN, for death shalt die but you shall live forever! DO NOT LIVE IN FEAR OF DEATH.

Now then, today and every day from now, choose to live!

Listen: *"So that as sin reigned in death, even so grace might reign through righteousness to eternal life through Jesus Christ our Lord." Romans 5:21-6:1*

Pray: Lord, I believe that in the future life, nothing dies. Dreams, relationships, ideas, desires, pets, and other companions, shall never die. There shall be no fear of loss, and we shall at last be free to enjoy Your life in all its infinite fullness! Oh but My Father, O my dear Jesus, help me to live in this life without the fear of death hanging over me. Amen and let it be so!

Night-Whisper | **DANGER**

Black Opium

F our expensive, exotic and imported substances, four aromatic 'spices,' were taken and then pounded together. Thus fused, they were then mixed with olive oil into a now bonded and exceptionally aromatic mass. This anointing oil was then further enhanced with a complimentary incense compound of sweet spices, so that the very atmosphere of the tabernacle surrounding the anointed tools, the garments and the priests, provided the olfactory senses of the worshippers with a unique fragrance of utter and unusual delight. Make no mistake about it, this compound of loveliness was not to be reproduced outside of the tabernacle nor used for anything but its Divine design or purpose. Nor was it to be placed upon the uncalled and the unholy. The penalty for doing so was banishment from the community of people of God and exclusion from the covenant of God as well. Now that's a patent penalty to take seriously!

Exodus 30:31-33

"And you shall speak to the children of Israel, saying: 'This shall be a holy anointing oil to Me throughout your generations. It shall not be poured on man's flesh; nor shall you make any other like it, according to its composition. It is holy, and it shall be holy to you. Whoever compounds any like it, or whoever puts any of it on an outsider, shall be cut off from his people.'"
NKJV

I wonder if there were four purposes for this total immersion anointing, which would mitigate such a serious patent infringement?

The first and important mundane purpose was no doubt that of replacing the smell of death. I love a bit of roast lamb friends, but the tabernacle was a place of permanent killing, even a vast abattoir killing factory which ran red with blood. The smell must have been shocking. Thus, to cover and camouflage the smell of death and the running blood, this sweetest perfume, in the form of anointing oil and the complimentary fragrance of incense, must have well and truly covered the smell of burnt offering and slit throat blood. I wonder if there was any disinfectant quality to any of this aroma?

Secondly, the reason for this patented perfume was no doubt one of 'total and specific recall.' In other words, I wonder if the uniqueness of this fragrance was to be used by God as a distinct and pin-point memory marker? When we breathe though our noise (the first and orthonasal way of smelling,) the olfactory neurons in the upper part of the nose generate an impulse which is passed to the brain along the olfactory nerve right to the brain's olfactory bulb, which then processes the signal and passes that information to the limbic system, which is a set of brain structures that scientists believe play a major role in controlling mood, behavior emotion, and memory. It is thought that the sense of smell is closely linked with memory probably more so than any of our other senses, especially because smells can trigger spontaneous recall! In other words, you don't even have to think about it. The smell immediately brings to mind all associated memories.

Thirdly, smell is also highly emotive. You should see the emotion of disgust on my wife's face when she comes across a pair of my well-worn socks or 'scuddy' underwear!

Thirdly, smell is also highly emotive. You should see the emotion of disgust on my wife's face when she comes across a pair of my well-worn socks or 'scuddy' underwear! Also, look at your media screens where the perfume industry is spending vast amounts of advertising money around this smelly memory connection, developing fragrances that seek to convey a vast array of emotions and feelings; from desire to power, vitality to relaxation and especially beauty, branding and sex! So much of this industry is producing fragrances associated with sin. Think about that. What do you see or smell when I say 'Opium, Elle, La Nuit, , Killer Queen, Deep Night, Cherish, Sweetheart, and a thousand more besides!' Smell is highly emotive, for it not only brings memories instantaneously to mind, but it moves the heart.

Fourthly, there had to be a unique smell which had total connection with 'holiness to the Lord' and blood sacrifice, even a perfume so uniquely pungent that it would not only move the mind in immediate remembrance but also move the heart in the offering of thankfulness for sin covered, and worship for grace given, as well as action in the fulfillment of vows taken.

So then, we must be careful not to compound any counterfeit perfume. We cannot create a plastic holiness or make, that is, fashion, a Jesus (for what is the tabernacle all about but Jesus!) which is a counterfeit compound to the beautiful fragrance and associated memory and emotions of that one and only unique perfume which is Christ. I tell you, we the modern church have not compounded a better 'Jesus of Nazareth,' but rather created some Cheeses of Nazareth! We have made a cheesy Jesus which fits into a compromised church and into a rebellious world. We have compounded a Jesus which is nothing but a stink! The result of this is nothing but cutting off of congregations from the covenant of blood. Our apostate apothecaries have remade God in our own acceptable image. They shall be cut off for God help us, they are cutting off millions from the fresh fragrance of Jesus. False anointing always leaves a skin rash, a blot on holy flesh and an allergic reaction around the ears which makes them itch. Friends, we have compounded a fallacy and then put it on strangers and sinners and called them 'Reverend, Pastors, Vicar' when they are nothing but stinkers. God will judge us for this. God is judging us for this.

We have compounded a fallacy and then put it on strangers and sinners and called them 'Reverend, Pastors, Vicar' when they are nothing but stinkers. God will judge us for this.

How will we know if we are anointed with this Divine perfume or some other substitute compound made by apostate apothecaries? Two ways. First of all, to those who are being saved, their testimony of us shall be that we are of a sweet perfume of life. To the rebel, to the reprobate, to the apostate, we shall simply stink of death and condemnation, of decomposition and slurried body fluids. Listen now, holiness is not to everyone's liking, taste nor savor. Brother, life your spiritual arm up and stick you snout in your armpit. How are you really smelling tonight?

Listen: *" So I came out to meet you, Diligently to seek your face, and I have found you. I have spread my bed with tapestry, colored coverings of Egyptian linen. I have perfumed my bed with myrrh, aloes, and cinnamon. Come, let us take our fill of love until morning; let us delight ourselves with love. For my husband is not at home; He has gone on a long journey; He has taken a bag of money with him, And will come home on the appointed day." With her enticing speech she caused him to yield, With her flattering lips she seduced him. Immediately he went after* *her, as an ox goes to the slaughter, Or as a fool to the correction of the stocks, Till an arrow struck his liver. As a bird hastens to the snare, He did not know it would cost his life. Now therefore, listen to me, my children; Pay attention to the words of my mouth: Do not let your heart turn aside to her ways, Do not stray into her paths; For she has cast down many wounded, And all who were slain by her were strong men. Her house is the way to hell, descending to the chambers of death. (Proverbs 7:15-27 NKJV)*

Pray: Father, how the false prophets have come out to meet your idiot children. Father, how the false perfume of a weak and insipid Jesus has filled the air around us. Father, how the lie of You not being at home, of You being gone on a long journey in a far country never to be around until the appointed day has allowed such open adultery. Therefore, cut in ribbons, O God, even those red lips of seducing flattery, cut them in ribbons and help us to be disgusted at the stench of that sweet compound of an illegally compounded 'knock off' of a Gospel. Lord, give us a nose for error and swift feet to run from it. Meanwhile O God, thank you that You lead us in triumph in Jesus and through us, diffuse the fragrance of His knowledge in every place. For we are to You O Lord the fragrance of Christ among those who are being saved and among those who are perishing. To the one we are the aroma of death leading to death, and to the other the aroma of life leading to life. And who is sufficient for these things? For we are not, as so many, peddling the word of God; but as of sincerity, but as from God, we speak in the sight of God in Christ. (adapted from 2 Cor 2:14-17 NKJV)

| Vol 02 | Q2 | NW00460 | April 03rd |

Night-Whisper | **HUMILITY**

The grace of overlooking

Nelson's column is the centerpiece of London. Even Trafalgar square in which it stands is a monument to his most famous of victories. One of the most repeated sayings of Lord Nelson is reputed to have first been uttered by him at the battle of Copenhagen, today in 1801. It was a furious naval action in which the British gunners are reported as "firing broadsides every 40 seconds and thus shrouding the whole scene in gun smoke." It was during this battle, that Lord Nelson famously turned a blind eye to an order from his commander in chief.

1 Samuel 14:43-45

And Jonathan told him, and said, "I only tasted a little honey with the end of the rod that was in my hand. So now I must die!" Saul answered, "God do so and more also; for you shall surely die, Jonathan." But the people said to Saul, "Shall Jonathan die, who has accomplished this great deliverance in Israel? Certainly not! As the Lord lives, not one hair of his head shall fall to the ground, for he has worked with God this day." So the people rescued Jonathan, and he did not die. NKJV

Apparently, Horatio Nelson was aboard HMS Elephant when a signal was clearly seen from his commander in chief's ship ordering Nelson's present action to cease! Nelson, who by now had only one arm and one eye, is reported to have put the telescope to his blind eye and said, "I really do not see the signal." His command to his then protesting lookout was very clear: "Mr.. Langford," he said, "I told you to look out on the Danish commodore and let me know when he surrendered; keep your eye fixed on him." In other words, Nelson overlooked the signal from his commander in chief to withdraw and continued to pummel the Danish ship into surrender. The consequent and continued close quarter's bombardment overwhelmed the enemy of the day and of course, resulted in yet another famous victory!

Jonathan son of Saul, had by God's hand, been right victorious and totally unaware of the command and oath of his father King Saul, that no one was to eat during the time of battle. *"Cursed is the man who eats any food until evening, before I have taken vengeance on my enemies." (1 Samuel 14:24-25)* So, Jonathan not knowing of the oath and the curse, had taken and eaten a little wild honey and so seemingly sealed his unfortunate fate. Saul, like Jephthah of old, had made a death-vow, and like Jephthah of old, his child Jonathan bore the brunt of it. There has to be a lesson there somewhere! However, for today let us note that as far as Saul was concerned, his son Jonathan must die. It's just plain bonkers!

The Scriptures present these incidents to us that we might see the stupidity of unbending men, that we might then take it to heart and make sure that we do not follow in their silly footsteps.

What went wrong here? Well, it is clear, is it not, that King Saul had made the wrong decision in depriving his troops of food for the fight? Jonathan knew that with the strength of such shining and sugary sustenance, Israel could have delivered themselves even more from the oppression of their enemies. In light of Jonathan's victories, Saul should have been humbled enough to speak clearly and honestly and just say to the people, "Oops!" Or, on the other hand, better still, like Nelson of old maybe, be wise and gracious to his conquering son and turn a blind eye to his previous orders and keep pounding the enemy?

The Scriptures present these incidents to us that we might see the stupidity of unbending men, that we might then take it to heart and make sure that we do not follow in their silly footsteps, for surely, it is easier in the face of victory to overlook both the thankful disobedience of those we might command and the rash words which we might have uttered in our own fear before the fray? If more leaders did this, then maybe then, we would all have more enjoyment in our well-fought fights and hard earned victories?

Listen: *"He who covers a transgression seeks love." Prov 17:9*

Pray: Lord, help me to know, when to confront and when to cover, that I may always seek love and foster victory with all accompanying joy! Help me to humble myself, help me to say 'Oops! I got it wrong.' In Jesus name I ask it, amen and let it be so.

| Vol 02 | Q2 | NW00461 | April 04th |

Night-Whisper | **STILLNESS**

These are hard ribs

Welsh poet RS Thomas in his poem 'In a Church' sums up our often shared, 20th century experience of silence.

Often I try
To analyze the quality of its silences.
Is this where God hides
From my searching? I have stopped to listen,
After the few people have gone
To the air recomposing itself
For vigil. It has waited like this
Since the stones grouped themselves about it.
These are hard ribs
Of a body that our prayers have failed
To animate. Shadows advance
From their corners to take possession
Of places that light held
For an hour. The bats resume
Their business. The uneasiness of the pews
Ceases.
There is no other sound
In the darkness but the sound of a man
Breathing, testing his faith
On emptiness, nailing his questions
One by one to an untenanted cross.

Psalm 46:10a

Be still, and know that I am God; NKJV

Friends, we are rarely ever alone in our silences are we? Bills, forgotten words, jobs, haste, hurry, desire, appetite, fidgets, fears, and fatigue, all sit noisily with us in our attempts at quietude. The only thing to do then, is to listen to their shouts until they die away in the distance of our thoughts. After their noisy and reluctant departure we often hear that which we fear nearly most of all; our own true voice. Maybe still a child, weeping, chiding us with neglect, longing to be listened to at last and pleading for release. Maybe a man ashamed of who he is, of who he has become. Maybe a woman full of hate and bad words toward herself, maybe a warrior who calls himself a coward, maybe... well you get my picture. It takes both time and silence to acquaint ourselves with ourselves doesn't it?

> *It takes both time and silence to acquaint ourselves with ourselves doesn't it?*

When we allow the louder noises to depart and the real voice of our self to speak, then maybe it will be then, in that eventual gentled and loving stillness, (for it is amazing how quiet it gets once our voices actually get a chance to finally be listened to,) that then He whom our soul loves and longs for, finally is also heard speaking to us! Maybe then at last, we shall truly begin to listen. So please, come "Speak Lord in the stillness, while we wait on Thee, hushed our hearts to listen, in expectancy."

"In Christian terms," British literary critic Tony Dyson explains, "Thomas is not a poet of the transfiguration, of the resurrection, of human holiness.... He is a poet of the Cross, the unanswered prayer, the bleak trek through darkness, and his theology of Jesus, in particular, seems strange against any known traditional norm." Anne Stevenson of the Listener describes Thomas as "a religious poet" who "sees tragedy, not pathos, in the human condition.... He is one of the rare poets writing today who never asks for pity." I like Thomas. An Anglican priest, a hard man, and as some have said, a rough man, realistic and merciless, a product of the Welsh valleys, its baled hilltops and lonely farms. He is familiar with the sound of silence and the products of ploughing alone in the bleak fields of quietness. Friend, you need to have courage enough to face the silence, even in an a deserted church.

So then, in this noisy world, neither fear death, not the silence of this life. Indeed, seek out silence, and plunge right in. Let the shouts die away, then listen to yourself. Listen to God. Get it sorted. Get to it.

Listen: *"....and after the fire a still small voice." 1 Kings 19:12-13*

Pray: Lord, help me not fear the silences of this life and the loud eternal voices it so often contains. Nor let me inadvertantly despise the quietness that You so often bring me as a gift.. Amen and let it be so.

Rupert Christiansen in the Telepgraph,writes that "John Greenleaf Whittier (1807-92) was an American Quaker who firmly believed that God was best worshipped in silent meditation and who deplored the histrionics associated with both the High Church and the Evangelical movement. However, he did allow these verses to be used in a hymn book published in 1884. Whittier advocated waiting instead for "the still small voice of calm" – an injunction beautifully suggested in the climax to its tune, Repton, composed by Hubert Parry."

Dear Lord and Father of mankind,
Forgive our foolish ways!
Re-clothe us in our rightful mind
In purer lives thy service find,
In deeper reverence praise.

In simple trust like theirs who heard,
Beside the Syrian sea,
The gracious calling of the Lord,
Let us, like them, without a word
Rise up and follow thee.

O Sabbath rest by Galilee!
O calm of hills above,
Where Jesus knelt to share with thee
The silence of eternity,
Interpreted by love!

With that deep hush subduing all
Our words and works that drown
The tender whisper of thy call,
As noiseless let thy blessing fall
As fell thy manna down.

Drop thy still dews of quietness
Till all our strivings cease;
Take from our souls the strain and stress,
And let our ordered lives confess
The beauty of thy peace.

Breathe through the heats of our desire
Thy coolness and thy balm;
Let sense be dumb, let flesh retire;
Speak through the earthquake, wind and fire,
O still small voice of calm!

Night-Whisper | **MERCY**

Dining with Dennis the hamster.

O utside in the darkness adjacent to a closed back door, underneath the low sill of an old damp window, I found my first fond pet, breathing badly and dying of a heart attack. I couldn't lift Lassie because she was so old and heavy, especially for a young lad like me, so I had to leave her there alone whilst I raced on home to get my father.

Deuteronomy 25:4

"You shall not muzzle an ox while it treads out the grain." NKJV

It was my first experience of death and I asked my dad, "Will Lassie be in heaven?" Indeed, this was the very same question which I also asked the Roman Catholic priest at one of my first confessions. My Father didn't know what to say and the priest just ignored me and gave me two "Our Fathers," and a "Hail Mary". I remember mumbling through my penance and was angry that God had no answer to the pain I felt in the loss of this lovely old dog. My first fond pet, found dead. Obviously, God did not care about dogs. I wonder if He cares about other pets?

Since then I have said goodbye to Patch my teenage hound, Marmalade our cat, and Dennis the hamster. I had great affection for each of them. It's amazing how much we get attached to little things. Tell me, "Will they be in heaven? Shall I see these lovely creatures again?"

Born in other countries mind you, these same companions of mine may have also been heartily and possibly thankfully delivered to my hungry stomach! If I ate them, would I see them then in heaven? Would I want to? Now there's a thought! Will we see each KFC we have devoured, and wow at each cow we have consumed? Will animals be redeemed? I mean, just how does God care about the animal kingdom? Are they but mere fun and fodder for those created in His image? William Blake in his Poem, "At the Last Judgment" writes: -

A dog starved at his masters gate
Predicts the ruin of the state

A horse misused upon the road
Cries to heaven for human blood

I have yet to see many works addressing God's relation to, and God's delight in, His very own animal kingdom. Mind you, I can understand the avoidance of the issue for I don't begin to understand the purpose of soft deer and hungry carnivores being placed on the same planet? Except that sin and bloody sacrifice are Scripturally speaking, always destined to walk hand in hand in this great story of ours, then the reason for the created and open ferocity, ripped skin and shed blood of the animal Kingdom eludes me. I can barely imagine what a redeemed animal Kingdom will look like, for I am sure there will be no more ripped and torn carcasses. If so, then surely then, the carrion we see now will be out of a job?

I can barely imagine what a redeemed animal Kingdom will look like, for I am sure there will be no more ripped and torn carcasses. If so, then surely then, the carrion we see now will be out of a job?

Nevertheless, I know Jesus ate fish, and at least once a year was partial to little roast lamb Himself. I know He rode on a donkey. I know He shall yet come with clouds descending, riding on a mighty white warhorse; I know His throne is surrounded by composite and fantastic creatures. I know He cuddles kittens and pats dogs, and loves His creation and calls them all very, very good, even at one point with Job of old, delighting in its created ferocity whilst pointing to some kind of dinosaur and shouting in glee, saying: ***"Behold Behemoth!"***

Yes indeed, we can say that God gets excited about His fantastic creation and that He has entrusted it to us, to use it, to utilize it, to tend it and especially, to respect it.

Will I see Dennis the hamster again? In the light of my God withholding no good thing and loving me immensely I think I have to say this to that question: "If I want to dine with Dennis the hamster in my heavenly home, then I believe I will!" I'm partial to a bit of lettuce. In the meantime, let us respect God's magnificent creation and remember the lines of William Blake when he says:

A dog starved at his masters gate

Predicts the ruin of the state
A horse misused upon the road
Cries to heaven for human blood

Listen: *"A righteous man regards the life of his animal."* Prov 12:10

Pray: Lord, for all your animals that You provide, we give you thanks and ask that you would endue in us, the proper respect and honor for this most glorious of Your creation, in Jesus name we pray, amen.

Night-Whisper | **TRUST**

From roadkill to rags and riches

Now then, the phrase in these verses which bothers me greatly tonight and which I want to look at, is this, "See, I have commanded a widow there to provide for you." This widow is no rich countess. She is no Lydia, she is no 'Josephine' at the right hand of Pharaoh with seven years of grain stored away. No, she is poverty stricken, and on the very verge of death herself. Therefore, the Lord's statement of "See, I have commanded a widow there to provide for you," is nothing short of ridiculous!

1 Kings 17:8-12

Then the word of the Lord came to him, saying, "Arise, go to Zarephath, which belongs to Sidon, and dwell there. See, I have commanded a widow there to provide for you." So he arose and went to Zarephath. And when he came to the gate of the city, indeed a widow was there gathering sticks. And he called to her and said, "Please bring me a little water in a cup, that I may drink." And as she was going to get it, he called to her and said, "Please bring me a morsel of bread in your hand." So she said, "As the Lord your God lives, I do not have bread, only a handful of flour in a bin, and a little oil in a jar; and see, I am gathering a couple of sticks that I may go in and prepare it for myself and my son, that we may eat it, and die." NKJV

Look now, for there is more! When I examine the text I see no indication whatsoever that the widow is expecting Elijah? Neither is there any indication that God had spoken to her, encouraged her, or commanded her. No, the commanded and prepared is literally getting ready to die! Therefore, how can God say to Elijah, "See, I have commanded a widow there to provide for you." It is ridiculous! However, He did.

Friends, this widow was handpicked by God. Indeed, Jesus in Luke 4:25-27 says " But I tell you truly, many widows were in Israel in the days of Elijah, when the heaven was shut up three years and six months, and there was a great famine throughout all the land; but to none of them was Elijah sent except to Zarephath, in the region of Sidon, to a woman who was a widow." Friends, she wasn't even a Jew and she resided in the area where the arch enemy of Elijah. Jezebel, had originated from. Watch how God shall prepare a table for his servant in the heart of his enemies country.

God sent Elijah on an 80-90 mile trek, to a place outside the covenant, to a person outside the covenant, even to an improbable source of supply in an impossible situation! Even so, this widow woman believed in the fact that Elijah's God was 'the living God!' There you go! That's it, she had an active faith in the present providence of an active and intervening God. She knew that God was the living God whose presence and practice interweaved all of life, and even her present tragedies of loss, paucity, poverty and famine. This widow was a woman of faith! And I wonder if she was the only one with the capacity to gamble the very last dregs of her life in believing that the living God could, and would supply here every daily need should He so wish. Might I suggest that she was the only one woman who could. The only one, and that's why Elijah was sent there! Think about that.

The widow woman knew that God was the living God whose presence and practice interweaved all of life, and even her present tragedies of loss, paucity, poverty and famine.

Elijah has been living a year on water and roadkill. If I was him I would be expecting a nice room at an Inn, and some decent food. Elijah was not disappointed at the state of this widow however, for he knew that the living God could, and would perpetuate the little into a miraculous and daily providence. He, the widow woman and her son, would live on the promises of God. Truly then, our eyes must be on the source of provision rather than not on the varying and often times unusual and troubling conduits of the same. Yes, our eyes must be upon Jehovah Jireh.

Even so, how was this widow 'commanded' in her becoming a provision toward Elijah? I think the commentator Matthew Henry has is right when he suggest that God made her both willing and able. Yes, God had appointed her to this place of provision and , prepared her heart for it, and also provided for the fulfillment of the task out of the remnants of her meagerness. In this way, God 'Commanded' a widow to provide for lonely Elijah, who had been 'buried alive' at the Brooke Cherith for the last year of his life.

Tonight, have your eyes on the source, and not the conduit, on the fountain and not the bucket! God will provide for you, and He shall use whatever agent and agency He desires to do so. Therefore do not turn your nose up at 'road-kill' nor be dismayed when ragged widows ready to die are willing to help you out of their meagerness. A blessed and believing heart, lasts longer and goes further than any bank account.

There are Christian charitable trusts today who have millions of money in their bank accounts. I fear for them that when the coming great accountant examines the bank balance in His balances, that he shall be greatly dismayed not to find it all spent on the cause of the Gospel. Friends, I shall this year attend maybe funerals of family members. You cannot take anything with you. Spend what you have and spend it well on that which is eternal. What might Elijah say to us tonight then? I think he might say this......

Listen: *Trust in the Lord with all your heart, And lean not on your own understanding; In all your ways acknowledge Him, And He shall direct your paths. (Proverbs 3:5-6 NKJV)*

Pray: Send the ravens Lord, and if You will, for a time, even bury me alive in silent obscurity and feed me with piecemeal meats and tidbits of bread dipped in clear, clear water. Send out the scavengers O Lord and scavenge for me. Send me faithful widows O God, and send me to them that I might be provided for, yes, send all Your agents of provision that I might live to fulfill Your will and purpose in my life Amen and let it be so.

Night-Whisper | **EXPECTATION**

Of giants and pillars of salt

A World War II correspondent once described the atmosphere of a room containing 35 men who had been assigned to a bombing mission from which, on average, 75% would not return. The correspondent noted that what he felt in those men, was not so much fear but "A profound reluctance to give up the future."

Philippians 3:82

Yet indeed I also count all things loss for the excellence of the knowledge of Christ Jesus my Lord. NKJV

Maybe, apart from the most ardent Hindus of the East, we in the West are very much creatures of the now and the near to now. Despite our weekly sermons, our daily quiet times, our Scripture memorization, our spiritual reading, our spiritual watching, we have still failed to become creatures possessed by an eternal vista. We do not set our hearts on things which are above, we do not invest in the unfading, neither do we only seek a heavenly city, who's builder and maker is God. A brief examination of our physical and psychological portfolios will give testimony to this, and in agreement to this statement of mine, all our psychosomatic illnesses shout a very large "Amen!"

I am at a loss to know what will change our vista up towards heaven, which is our eternal home? Maybe only the onset of a terminal illness will do it. It is a frightening thought is not it. However, the joke is on us, for we all, this side of the renewal, already have a terminal illness! Yes, we are all passing through, we are all going to die, yet we continue to look down and not look up. This world is nothing but giant cemetery so why are we building in it. The more I think about this, the more it just seems to be plain craziness!

The prospect of leaving your earthly lover, your dearly loved ones and committing them to an unknown future, maybe involving the care and happiness of another earthly lover, another stand in father or mother, does indeed wrench any human heart. Add to this the inability that such a departure brings in being unable to achieve your own heart's desires for the coming years; robbing you of your dreams, career and the opportunity to taste the fruit of the work of your own hands, yes, when you add all these things together, they do indeed make death a very bitter pill to swallow. Therefore I believe the war correspondent was correct in that "The sense of loss, the seeming senseless waste, the robbery of life and future that death brings with it, is a fiercer giant than the fear of death itself."

These two giants, suffering death and fearful loss will not go away. They are still heavily armed, bludgeon practiced fiends that stand each side of the gates to any temporal happiness..

These two giants, *suffering death* and *fearful loss* will not go away. They are still heavily armed, bludgeon practiced fiends that stand each side of the gates to any temporal happiness. However, it seems to me that their power is only felt, is only effective in destruction, when we simply stand there and stare into their all-consuming eyes.

Friends, this morning, today and tomorrow then, commit not to look into the eyes of these giants, for the fact is, they are defeated foes and have no power over the Christian, that is, unless we insist in meeting their terrible gaze and then just stand in front of them to be bludgeoned, beaten into a pillar of salt. A million statuesque pillars of Christian salt all give testimony to this. Too many of our tribe have longed after a happier Egypt and gazed back through the temporal gates of Sodom, only to meet the dreadful eyes of these two giants only to then be left bludgeoned and lifeless in the desert!

We have some major adjustments to make dear friends and mostly they are in our neck. Look up! Wherever you are today, look up! Ignore those giant twins, for they have no power over you.

Listen: *"Then the LORD rained brimstone and fire on Sodom and Gomorrah, from the LORD out of the heavens. So He overthrew those cities, all the plain, all the inhabitants of the cities, and what grew on the ground. But his wife looked back behind him, and she became a pillar of salt." Genesis 19:24-26 NKJV*

"Yet indeed I also count all things loss for the excellence of the knowledge of Christ Jesus my Lord, for whom I have suffered the loss

of all things, and count them as rubbish, that I may gain Christ."
Philippians 3:8-9

"...and let us run with endurance the race that is set before us, looking unto Jesus, the author and finisher of our faith, who for the joy that was set before Him endured the cross, despising the shame, and has sat down at the right hand of the throne of God." Hebrews 12:1-2

We have some major adjustments to make dear friends and mostly they are in our neck. Look up!

"By faith he dwelt in the land of promise as in a foreign country, dwelling in tents with Isaac and Jacob, the heirs with him of the same promise; for he waited for the city which has foundations, whose builder and maker is God." Hebrews 11:9-10

"But you, beloved, building yourselves up on your most holy faith, praying in the Holy Spirit, keep yourselves in the love of God, looking for the mercy of our Lord Jesus Christ unto eternal life." Jude 20-21

Pray: Help me O Lord, to set my eyes on things above and help me not to allow myself to gaze into the eyes of these defeated but most terrible of giants. Amen.

Night-Whisper | **FIGHT**

Wrap rage

Goods and gifts now purchased by us all are so securely packaged that there is rarely any chance of damage in either transportation or distribution. The problem is that for the average bear, getting into these things can be a formidable problem! Broken nails, chipped teeth, pulled out hair, and in 2003, in the United Kingdom, 67,000 visits to the emergency department of local hospitals are testimony to what has become known as "wrap rage"! I am sure that it will come of no surprise to many of you when I tell you that the Bible has always presented its greatest surprises tightly wrapped and that they too have caused some horrific problems, even some terrifying wrap rage, if you will.

Luke 2:122

And this will be the sign to you: "You will find a Babe wrapped in swaddling cloths, lying in a manger."
NKJV

From the fall of man in the garden of Eden when the promise of the EWF (Eternal Wrestling Federation) champion, the Head Crusher, was given as a light and a hope to Adam and to all of us so genetically bound up in him, a struggle of gigantic proportions has been taking place. Time and again, from the slaying of Abel, through the attempted, fallen angelic corruption of humanity and the destruction of Messianic Kingdoms, the enemy has tried to thwart the arrival of the promise, the Messiah, the Savior, the Redeemer, the lovely, the beautiful, majestic, desirable, honorable, worthy, King, Master and Shepherd, the Good, the One and only, the Son of God, Prince Jesus! Yup, as soon as this promise was given, the cry went up from the ring announcer, "Let's get ready to rumble!"

The enemy failed to stop the arrival of the promise and failed most thoroughly at trying to thwart His mission! However, his rage is still very great. Bunyan was correct when personifying our enemy as Apollyon the Destroyer, who when facing Christian walking in the will of God, comes against him breaking into "A grievous rage, saying, 'I am an enemy to this Prince; I hate His person, His laws, and people: I am come out on purpose to withstand thee'." Fear not these all too familiar ad dreadfully felt words dear friends, and don't cringe in cowardice aft his fiery bombast, but rather, let your heart beat in time with Bunyan's Christian when he replies, "Apollyon, beware what you do, for I am in the King's highway, the way of holiness; therefore take heed to yourself." My fellow Christian, if you are on the way of Holiness today then you need not fear the injuries of any Satanic wrap rage. He needs to fear you!

> *My fellow Christian, if you are on the way of Holiness today then you need not fear the injuries of any Satanic wrap rage. He needs to fear you!*

Listen: *"Then did Christian draw, for he saw it was time to bestir him; and Apollyon as fast made at him, throwing darts as thick as hail; by the which, notwithstanding all that Christian could do to avoid it, Apollyon wounded him in his head, his hand, and foot. This made Christian give a little back; Apollyon, therefore, followed his work amain, and Christian again took courage, and resisted as manfully as he could. This sore combat lasted for above half a day, even till Christian was almost quite spent; for you must know that Christian, by reason of his wounds, must needs grow weaker and weaker.*

"Then Apollyon, espying his opportunity, began to gather up close to Christian, and wrestling with him, gave him a dreadful fall; and with that Christian's sword flew out of his hand. Then said Apollyon, I am sure of thee now. And with that he had almost pressed him to death, so that Christian began to despair of life; but as God would have it, while Apollyon was fetching of his last blow, thereby to make a full end of this good man, Christian nimbly stretched out his hand for his sword, and caught it, saying, 'Rejoice not against me, O mine enemy; when I fall I shall arise;' and with that gave him a deadly thrust, which made him give back, as one that had received his mortal wound. Christian perceiving that, made at him again, saying, 'Nay, in all these things we are more than conquerors through him that loved us.' And with that Apollyon spread forth his dragon's wings, and sped him away, that Christian for a season saw him no more.

"In this combat no man can imagine, unless he had seen and heard as I did, what yelling and hideous roaring Apollyon made all the time of the fight - he spake like a dragon; and, on the other side, what sighs and groans burst from Christian's heart. I never saw him all the while give so

much as one pleasant look, till he perceived he had wounded Apollyon with his two-edged sword; then, indeed, he did smile, and look upward; but it was the dreadfullest sight that ever I saw... Then there came to him a hand, with some of the leaves of the tree of life, the which Christian took, and applied to the wounds that he had received in the battle, and was healed immediately. He also sat down in that place to eat bread, and to drink of the bottle that was given him a little before; so, being refreshed, he addressed himself to his journey, with his sword drawn in his hand; for he said, I know not but some other enemy may be at hand."

Pray: Lord, help me to be a true resistance fighter, amen.

Night-Whisper | **ACTION**

'Participation in Public life,' or, 'The care of your enemy's donkey'

It used to be said 'never speak about politics or religion' in a pub as it would undoubtedly offend some people and might even cause arguments. However, when people get a few drinks in them, I find that it seems they can talk about little else. Why is this? It is because politics and religion divide people, and force them to defend their position and attack those who oppose them. This is the human condition, and alcohol, removes the inhibitions of cultural politeness and leads people to investigate the divide.

Exodus 23:1-5

"You shall not circulate a false report. Do not put your hand with the wicked to be an unrighteous witness. You shall not follow a crowd to do evil; nor shall you testify in a dispute so as to turn aside after many to pervert justice. You shall not show partiality to a poor man in his dispute. "If you meet your enemy's ox or his donkey going astray, you shall surely bring it back to him again. If you see the donkey of one who hates you lying under its burden, and you would refrain from helping it, you shall surely help him with it. NKJV

The legacy church and its leaders have longed since stop talking about politics and comparative religion at the small-talks lecterns. Why? Because their charity status is legally tied up in restrictions of not presenting 'political party bias' or 'political party promotion,' and also the greater fact that a good percentage of their politically mixed congregations will be offended and will leave, taking their cash with them. The result is silenced prophets for profit's sake.

Politics does not really divide. No, humanity is essentially divided along four lines (and in this order,) money, health, intellect, and religion. Politics is simply an expression of these four fault lines of division.

Money divides people. At a massive extreme, the January 2016 Davos report by Oxfam says that 62 people in the world own the same as half the world combined! To make it worse for the PC socialists, 53 of these are men and 9 are women. I understand the 9 women are pursuing a 'gender inequality in wages' legal suit against the 53 men. The Oxfam report goes on to say that the wealth of 1% of the world's population is equal to the rest of the world's 99% combined. These are stunning facts. Utterly astounding! my God, let us set boundaries to the acquisition and hoarding of earthly riches. Indeed, let those who exceed those set, be then shunned by society. We give power to the mega-rich, when we bow down and serve them. STOP IT! Let us shun them. Let us shame them.

"Here's an acre sown indeed with the richest royallest seed

that the earth did e'er suck in, since the first man died for sin:

Here the bones of birth have cried, "Though gods they were, as men they died!"

At the moment, I think I am a Sepulcharian, libertarian, caring, capped, free market capitalist. I believe in the duty of all men to work, and to have the opportunity to do so. I believe in the right for all men to become rich through their work. I define basic earthly richness in the presence of a peace, a permanent roof, table, and the means to put food upon it. Simple really. The existence of government is for a fourfold purpose, that being to protect those who do good according to God's law, to punish those who do evil, to protect its citizens against those who steal its homeland peace, and finally, to provide an atmosphere, an ecosphere, for the freedom to work and make money. It is the duty of families to take care of their own poor. This falls primarily to earthly families and secondly to church families. It is then the duty of local communities to aid the poor in being able to eventually provide for themselves. Where this is not possible, let those who possess beyond the basics of riches in this worlds goods help them to do so.

You undoubtedly have a political opinion and stance. If you don't, then go out and get one immediately! Our text for tonight is an imperative for justice and activity in all manner of public life, even the care of your enemies donkey. Your political position may well be different to mine. That's OK. For a multitude of safe and sane reasons, division is a good thing. Even so, whatever the description of your political position is, you are currently a Sepulcharian. And this word should prefix all political descriptors.

One commentator rightly said that Abraham bought one piece of land when he was alive on this earth and at the bottom of that particular field was a sepulcher for his bones and the bones of his family. Presently, we all die in the end. This body, your body, is destined for dissolution. We came into this world naked and we shall leave it in the same way. Life ends in death, and death leads to judgement. Did I tell you that presently I think I am Sepulcharian, libertarian, caring, capped, free market capitalist? However, above all, I am a Sepulcharian.

Politics cannot change nor prosper the world. It can only keep sin in some kind of check before the cleansing of Christ shall come. Do not kid yourselves, for there is no utopia to be made without the presence and rule of the King of Kings.

Get some politics in you! Get active. But know this, 'all things end in judgement,' including your part in politics and the care of your enemy's donkey, or not, as such the case may be.

Listen:

MORTALITY, behold and fear
What a change of flesh is here!
Think how many royal bones
Sleep within these heaps of stones;
Here they lie, had realms and lands,
Who now want strength to stir their hands,
Where from their pulpits seal'd with dust
They preach, "In greatness is no trust."
Here's an acre sown indeed
With the richest royallest seed
That the earth did e'er suck in
Since the first man died for sin:
Here the bones of birth have cried,
"Though gods they were, as men they died!"
Here are sands, ignoble things,
Dropt from the ruin'd sides of kings:
Here's a world of pomp and state
Buried in dust, once dead by fate.

'On the Tombs in Westminster Abbey,' by F. Beaumont.

Pray: Father, help us hold the political line so that the harvest of souls may be in freedom be fully brought in. Then come Great King, come quick, come soon, for with Your absence, the earth doth swoon. Even so, come Lord Jesus. Amen and let it be so.

Night-Whisper | **PRAISE**

An old song and a new national anthem

A s Scotland still and currently continues its push towards a socialist independence from the rest of the UK, which without further collapse of the oil industry, I think they will eventually get, the presence of an overwhelming number of Scottish National Party MP's in the house of commons, means that there has been a call for all things English rather than all things British to come to the fore to now respect what is the majority of people in these Islands. Votes for English MP's only on English matters, has now given way to the long cry for a truly English National Anthem. 'God Save Our Gracious Queen/King' just won't do anymore. It would appear that we are down to the wire on two tunes for the English National Anthem and that is, 'Land of Hope and Glory' and 'Jerusalem.' To be honest, both are national mocking jokes to me, but if I had a choice it would be 'Jerusalem,' and that purely for the opportunity to proclaim Christ on the back of it. I think it would be great for a future British Islamic state to have Blake's Jerusalem as a National Anthem. How wonderful.

Isaiah 62:1-2

For Zion's sake I will not hold My peace, And for Jerusalem's sake I will not rest, Until her righteousness goes forth as brightness, And her salvation as a lamp that burns. The Gentiles shall see your righteousness, And all kings your glory. You shall be called by a new name, Which the mouth of the Lord will name. NKJV

A national Anthem unites a people. National unity is a great and glorious thing. The globalists can't stand it mind you, but they can do take a running jump. Europas 'Ode to Joy,' a non-verbal anthem of unity and brotherhood for the European Union has been turned into the 'odorous jogging' of the speediest planned migration you've ever seen!

Even so, I am looking forward to the National Anthem of the body of Christ in heaven. Who shall write the words, the tune and how and on what occasions shall it be sung? Most certainly, the eternal National Anthem of the redeemed people of God shall be a fantastic thing to hear. Imagine, a unifying pride filled universe shaking rendition of the glories of Christ. I cannot wait to hear it and sing it.

In my mind, for the individual national unity of the temporal tribal peoples of God on earth, for the church militant in all their tongues, each should have their own Christian National Anthem. Therefore, may O be so bold as to suggest a Church Militant National Anthem for the English speaking peoples of the West? It is an obvious choice for sure, but allow me to put forward my reasons for choosing it.

The anthem should be eternally Nationalistic. It should speak of our own heavenly land of the great City above, even the city of all, free men, Jerusalem the beautiful, Jerusalem the golden, Jerusalem the free!

It should be written by an acknowledge by great man of God. A man full of the Scriptures and dedicated to reality and to truth, to humanity and to divinity. I believe the church has found this man.

The anthem should be eternally Nationalistic. It should speak of our own heavenly land of the great City above, even the city of all, free men, Jerusalem the beautiful, Jerusalem the golden, Jerusalem the free!

The anthem should be rousing, passionate, uniting, able to be sung without musical accompaniments, because the joined voices of singing become essentially its own accompaniment. It should be manly, warlike, for whatever a man can happily sing about, so can a woman. However, not many men can nor want to sing like a woman or what a woman might like to sing about. Surely, all the current 'Jesus is my girlfriend' songs which have contributed to the emptying of the church of true manliness should give testimony to that?

The anthem should glorify and magnify our great God, and extol His good and loving righteous rule and unstoppable sovereignty. It should be a song of certain rescue, a song of present provision and a song of constant joy, even a song of hope and home, of journeying and ecstatic expectant arrival there. This National Anthem should be another worldly song.

Yes, the church must rid itself of effeminate songs, of songs for performers instead of songs for the marching men of the congregation.

Friends, there is a song I recommend to you as the National Anthem for the English speaking tribe of the church militant in the Western lands. Here it is....

Listen: *You shall also be a crown of glory In the hand of the Lord, And a royal diadem In the hand of your God. You shall no longer be termed Forsaken, Nor shall your land any more be termed Desolate; But you shall be called Hephzibah, and your land Beulah; For the Lord delights in you, And your land shall be married. For as a young man marries a virgin, So shall your sons marry you; And as the bridegroom rejoices over the bride, So shall your God rejoice over you. I have set watchmen on your walls, O Jerusalem; They shall never hold their peace day or night. You who make mention of the Lord, do not keep silent, And give Him no rest till He establishes And till He makes Jerusalem a praise in the earth. (Isaiah 62:1-2 NKJV)*

Pray:

Come, we that love the Lord,
And let our joys be known;
Join in a song with sweet accord,
Join in a song with sweet accord
And thus surround the throne,
And thus surround the throne.

(Refrain) We're marching to Zion,
Beautiful, beautiful Zion;
We're marching upward to Zion,
The beautiful city of God.

The sorrows of the mind
Be banished from the place;
Religion never was designed
Religion never was designed,
To make our pleasures less,
To make our pleasures less.

Refrain

Let those refuse to sing,
Who never knew our God;
But favorites of the heavenly King,
But favorites of the heavenly King

May speak their joys abroad,
May speak their joys abroad.

Refrain

The God that rules on high,
And thunders when He please,
Who rides upon the stormy sky,
Who rides upon the stormy sky,
And manages the seas,
And manages the seas.

Refrain

This awful God is ours,
Our Father and our Love;
He will send down his heav'nly powers,
He will send down his heav'nly powers,
To carry us above,
To carry us above.

Refrain

There we shall see His face,
And never, never sin!
There, from the rivers of His grace,
There, from the rivers of His grace,
Drink endless pleasures in,
Drink endless pleasures in.

Refrain

Yea, and before we rise,
To that immortal state,
The thoughts of such amazing bliss,
The thoughts of such amazing bliss,
Should constant joys create,
Should constant joys create.

Refrain

The men of grace have found,
Glory begun below.
Celestial fruits on earthly ground
Celestial fruits on earthly ground

From faith and hope may grow,
From faith and hope may grow.

Refrain

The hill of Zion yields
A thousand sacred sweets
Before we reach the heav'nly fields,
Before we reach the heav'nly fields,
Or walk the golden streets,
Or walk the golden streets.

Refrain

Then let our songs abound,
And every tear be dry;
We're marching through Immanuel's ground,
We're marching through Immanuel's ground,
To fairer worlds on high,
To fairer worlds on high.

Refrain

Yoga, and other twisted games

Ken Blalock on his review of Dr. Tucker Calloway's book, *Zen Way- Jesus Way*, accuses him and all born again Christians who claim to know the truth as committing *"A sin at the altar of philosophy"* and he goes on to say that "meaningful dialogue is only possible when dogmatic thinking is put aside." May I offer what I consider an experiential translation of this very Eastern and yet postmodern point of view? Here it is, "It is a sin of utter arrogance to claim to know the truth. It is intolerance incarnate. It is offensive. It is death to dialogue." The absolutes of the Bible are absolutely not allowed in any inter-faith dialogue.

John 18:37-38

Pilate therefore said to Him, "Are You a king then?" Jesus answered, "You say rightly that I am a king. For this cause I was born, and for this cause I have come into the world, that I should bear witness to the truth. Everyone who is of the truth hears My voice." Pilate said to Him, "What is truth?"NKJV

You see, postmodern pilgrims pleasure themselves on Pilate's pontificating, munching on it as a meaningful meditative morsel and regurgitating it, until it becomes as anemic and as ineffective in providing direction and help, as it was to the man himself who first proposed the question just before a multitude saw him wash his hands of the very life blood of the answer to his pre-post-modern query of of, "What is truth?"

Christ never commanded his disciples to participate in a ministry of dialogue! He armed His followers with authority and power and sent them on a deliverance mission into enemy territory to plunder the strong man's goods. How are we doing friends, as we consume Café Grande's by the bucket load in communal coffee houses adjacent to hot yoga studios springing up in all the hip and happening places of this not so happy land of ours? A few lines from David Gray's song "The Space Between", maybe sums up well the expressions of all the fretting and frowning furrows of Western questioners that have almost dialogued themselves to death and still not found what they have been looking for:

These fickle, fuddled words confuse me.
Like "Will it rain today?"
Waste the hours with talking, talking.
These twisted games we're playing

Let's get real friends, for in the space between all the talking, the words of Christians alone, only make the sound of one hand clapping in the ears of postmodern pilgrims. For there is no thunder in our voice and no lightening in our living, nor any more longing in our looking! We do not seek a better country, for frankly, we like the one we have here, thank you very much indeed. No, the once valued possession of our words have been in recession, a long, long time.

Walkers of the way should tingle with truth and over flow with life, because they possess, and are possessed by Him who is indeed, the way, the truth, and the life!

I speak only for myself when I say, unless what I claim to possess is manifest in my life, it will not mean a fig to postmodern pilgrims for it's not defensive dialogue that will convince them, nor anemic apologies but a real demonstration of unquestioning resurrection power which is unrelentingly manifest in our lives. Walkers of the way should tingle with truth and over flow with life, because they possess, and are possessed by Him who is indeed, the way, the truth, and the life!

Deliverance is the answer and not dialogue but if we do not have the goods of our deliverance, then how can we help them with theirs? Yes, until we have the goods, it is probably best to keep our cakehole shut, lest we tire our listeners out with the sound of but one hand clapping.

How about you pilgrim? What's in your rucksack.

Listen: *"For the kingdom of God is not in word but in power." 1 Cor 4:20*

Pray: Come in love, come in gentleness, but come in resurrection power O Lord my God today, in Jesus name I pray, amen.

Night-Whisper | **TOUCH**

Touching lepers

In my personnel report, which was submitted to the human resources department, I recommended him for "sincere consideration for any job openings within the company." Indeed, I encouraged the company concerned to take him on by writing "As soon as a vaccine exists, I recommend that you employ him." Of course, I had meant to say vacancy What a difference the addition a small consonant can make to a phrase!

Leviticus 13:45,46

"Now the leper on whom the sore is, his clothes shall be torn and his head bare; and he shall cover his moustache, and cry, 'Unclean! Unclean!' He shall be unclean. All the days he has the sore he shall be unclean. He is unclean, and he shall dwell alone; his dwelling shall be outside the camp." NKJV

The spell checker took me from vacancy to vaccine in one fell swoop. That is my case your honor and I'm sticking to it! Spell checkers aren't that clever after all, but then again neither am I. By the way, they never did ask me what disease I thought he had, or how infectious he was. Maybe it didn't matter. Thankfully, it doesn't matter to Jesus either; He was and is very familiar with the touching of lepers.

The cruel and crippling desensitizing and disfiguring nature of leprosy, from the beginning has led it to be a despicable picture of the internal corruption that sin besets us all with. Most of us are aware of this within us but live in such a denial of its all-pervading influence, that we function on the level of cynical comparisons saying, "Well, I'm not as bad as her," or "I could be worse, like him over there" and "It's not that bad really." From early years, we have all been trying to change the habit, improve the propensity, and practice pleasant-hood, all in an attempt to remove the leprous spot from us. It cannot be done. I wonder maybe, if we need to see the horror of it more, or be more filled with the stench of it, or have it consume us and eat us up a little bit more, before we lay aside our pride and go running to Jesus, in desperation for help and healing. You know, I see desperation more and more, as a divine gift.

Maybe the most merciful one we could ever receive. Luke, the doctor, tells us of a man in a certain city, full of leprosy who ran to Jesus and said *"If you are willing you can make me clean."* Tell me, how full of leprous sin do you see yourself today? Where are you running to for help?

Listen: *"Then He put out His hand and touched him, saying, 'I am willing; be cleansed.' Immediately the leprosy left him." Luke 5:13*

Pray: Thank You that You are more willing to heal me, than I am to be healed. Reach, touch, and cleanse me today, oh my Savior, for You are my only hope. Amen.

Night-Whisper | **PREPARE**

Christian complacency, the sin of our age

In a world flooded with information, there is absolutely no excuse for the Christian to be uninformed. Oh for sure, there is a great chance to be ill-informed but not uninformed. Information needs to be panned so that the golden facts might be gathered together and then fashioned into objective truth. These glittering truths then need to be taken to God in prayer and scriptural consideration. This takes time, effort, contemplation and prayerful mediation.

There are three reason why Christians do not pan for golden facts in the world wide information streams. The first is a lack of time, the second is a lack of seen necessity, and this is based on the third reason, that is, the presence of unreasonable and unfounded trust. Yes, we trust the main news outlets to provide us with digested facts applied without spin and agenda into objective truths. We pride ourselves in the unbiased reporting of our own free press. What a load of old cobblers!

It is well past the time for people to wake up the fact that our main news outlets

Hosea 4:1-6

Hear the word of the Lord, You children of Israel, For the Lord brings a charge against the inhabitants of the land:" There is no truth or mercy Or knowledge of God in the land. By swearing and lying, Killing and stealing and committing adultery, They break all restraint, With bloodshed upon bloodshed. Therefore the land will mourn; And everyone who dwells there will waste away With the beasts of the field And the birds of the air; Even the fish of the sea will be taken away. "Now let no man contend, or rebuke another; For your people are like those who contend with the priest. Therefore you shall stumble in the day; The prophet also shall stumble with you in the night; And I will destroy your mother. My people are destroyed for lack of knowledge. Because you have rejected knowledge, I also will reject you from being priest for Me; Because you have forgotten the law of your God, I also will forget your children. NKJV are manned by turncoats. These politically correct and psychologically groomed gangsters of information, act according to the desires and intents of their owners, be they individuals, movements, interest groups, governments, or a mixture of all four of the above. All water taken from these streams needs purifying. If you are after the unbiased facts, the main news media outlets are not the place to find them. Pan their streams

I am a Bible believing Christian. I am part of the biggest conspiracy construct that has ever existed.

for golden facts, but do not believe a word they say about objective truth. Find out the truth for yourself.

I am a Bible believing Christian. I am part of the biggest conspiracy construct that has ever existed. The charge of being a 'Conspiracy Theorist' then, does neither shame me nor move me. My response is that I deal in conspiracy fact, not theory. Complacent Christianity, in a world flooded with information and luciferin declaration is still picnicking on the Somme. I tell you, there is a need for panic not a picnic! Let me then sound the alarm and command that you wake up brother and take a good look at what is actually happening to the church of the living God! While you are asleep, the removal van is at your door and a gang of thieves are piling in the contents of your dwelling including all your hidden treasures. Yet you think you are safe? I tell you, "you are not," for the gathered and objective truth points to your near demise. Why you trusting those who hate you, to provide you with the truth of what is actually going on? Why do you still believe that your 'nation' will take care of you?

Christian, the government will not take care of you or your family. Christian, society will not take care of you or your family. Christian, your employer will not take care of you or your family. Christian, social services will not take care of you or your family. Christian, the political parties will not take care of you or your family. Christian, the banks and your finances in them, will not take care of you or your family. Christian, the legacy church will not take care of you or your family! Christian, only God can take care of you, and on a good day, the body of Christ, the organized and prepared church militant, might just do the same.

The sin of the age is the complacency of the compromised church, and the lukewarmness of the sleeping and chosen ignorant who believe the guards at the camp will bring them dinner and keep the heating turned on. It's beyond ridiculous.

The end times Christian must become a two edged student. First of the Scriptures and secondly of the complexities and changes of the present age. There has never been a time like this (save in the days of Noah and the rising of old Babylon) in terms of technical innovation and conjoined demonic activity, as all God given boundaries have now been pulled down, violated, overturned and pushed into oblivion. Christians need to wake up to this and become students of the Scriptures and the present age. This takes time and effort. Therefore, Christians must now fully engage with the information streams to pan for the golden facts and construct the objective truth of what is happening in the light of God's Holy word. At the coming judgement seat of Christ, the answer to God of "Lord, I just did not know" shall in fact turn out to be "Lord, I just did not care enough." Friend, do you care enough to find out what's really going on? Or are you happy to have your house emptied, as long as you are not disturbed or hurt. Look now, for I tell you, that you shall be the last item to be loaded into the back of the truck. Asleep, or otherwise, they will at last come for you. Wake up Christian and engage with the Scriptures and a study of the present age.

Listen: *Do not remove the ancient landmark Which your fathers have set. (Proverbs 22:28 NKJV)*

Pray: Father, wake me up, God the Holy Spirit, shake me up, Lord Jesus Christ my master, stir me up to action. Father, Your boundaries of morality and spiritual investigation have been violated and moved, removed and destroyed. Inhumanity is breaking out all around us. Father, help us to know the truth of what is going on and the facts and the timetable of Your great unfolding plan. Unseal Your bound up words that we seekers of truth and the knowledge of Your coming, and the signs of Your appearing might know and might properly plan and greatly prepare. In Jesus name we ask it, amen and let it be so.

Night-Whisper | **FIGHT**

Taking care of business

"**E**very subject's duty is the King's; but every subject's soul is his own." So goes the reply of Henry V to Williams on the night before the battle of Agincourt. It's one my favorite plays, and in Act IV the dialogue Shakespeare places into the mouth of King Harry seems to have the hard-core base of the Scriptures about it. It's just marvelous!

Ephesians 6:10-12

Finally, my brethren, be strong in the Lord and in the power of His might...for we do not wrestle against flesh and blood.NKJV

Reading through the Acts of the Apostles, that brief history of the early church, shows very clearly that in the beginning, rather than there being a glorious appearing of the new body of Christ, the church militant here on earth was never a gentle coalescing of various friendly folk calmly stepping forth on the errands of their Master but rather, it was and seems to continue to be, more like the coming of a startled and struggling child that arrives kicking and screaming in the world. Herod it appears is still out to destroy the birth of this baby, and Rachel is still weeping for her children and the battle, ever rages in its great ferocity, in and around, over and under the true church of the living God.

The true church is a movement forged in fire, a body that is bathed in blood and battle. In the early days, the church's overall and main strategy appears to be that of survival! It is hard to discern much else on the mess of a battlefield, when the nature of such fighting dictates flexibility and imposes on its Commander and His generals the need for dynamic response to stay alive! Has this early survival state of mind continued I wonder?

In my opinion, the strategy for the global making of disciples lies totally in the heart of the sender, which is in turn, imparted of necessity into the hearts of those which are sent. So looking at the post Pentecost rise of a multitude of many different men, missionary movements and methods over the centuries, it is obvious that our Commander has had a flexible strategy to meet the needs of the hour. His strategy may change and we must be mindful and obedient to it, yet one thing never changes and that is the need to guard and maintain our own heart and the fire He has imparted to us. That is the pre-eminent thing to do in this battle, in this walk, in this journey in this mess of a fight, "keep your own heart and keep the home fires burning!" Today, remember brother and sister knight, these two great Shakespearian thoughts, which I believe are rooted in the Scriptures "Self-love, my liege, is not so vile a sin as self-neglecting." (King Henry V. Act ii. Sc. 4.) and "Every subject's duty is the Kings and every subject's soul is his own."

> *"Self-love, my liege, is not so vile a sin as self-neglecting."*

If I may elucidate a little further then, in this battle, our personal responsibility is twofold:

First, we must take care of business, we must take responsibility with Jesus for our own sacrifice, service and sanctification. In other words, we must work out our own salvation with fear and trembling. We must put Him first for every man's duty is the King's. Tell me today then, who's your daddy? Who's your lover? Who's your friend?

Secondly, and speaking as a protestant, we must do is take to heart the wise advice of our most blessed sister Mary:

Listen: *"His mother said to the servants, 'Whatever He says to you, do it.'" John 2:5*

Pray: Lord, I am a servant and soldier for the working day. Please Lord help me to be attentive to Your orders for this my day and help me to keep my own spirit soul and body, fit and hot, yes, ready to do Your will! Amen.

Night-Whisper | **BELIEVE**

The open grave, the open coffin and the closed room

N ow then, King Hezekiah's life was spared a further fifteen years and from his active loins sprang the monster, King Mannesah, who so angered and offended the Lord, that the whole nation was summarily destroyed. The moral of the story surely being, "be careful what you ask for."

Luke 8:50-56

But when Jesus heard it, He answered him, saying, "Do not be afraid; only believe, and she will be made well." When He came into the house, He permitted no one to go in except Peter, James, and John, and the father and mother of the girl. Now all wept and mourned for her; but He said, "Do not weep; she is not dead, but sleeping." And they ridiculed Him, knowing that she was dead. But He put them all outside, took her by the hand and called, saying, "Little girl, arise." Then her spirit returned, and she arose immediately. And He commanded that she be given something to eat. And her parents were astonished, but He charged them to tell no one what had happened. NKJV

The second of Christ's three miracles of resurrecting the dead was that of the only son of the widow of Nain (Luke 7:11-17). When Jesus, His entourage and the following crowd arrived, they met the sad funeral procession at the gate of the city. The living were going in, the dead were being carried out. The widow asked nothing of Jesus, but He, having compassion on the bereaving mother said to her, "Do not weep," and touching the open coffin, said to the corpse, "Young man, I say to you arise." We don't know what he said, but the corpse sat up in the coffin and started speaking. There was no hiding this great miracle, and indeed, 'this report about Him (of the miracle and of him being an undoubtedly great prophet) went throughout all Judea and all the surrounding region. This was spectacular advertising!

Three 'stages' of death were dealt with in Christs miracles: Lastly, the four day stinking stage of Lazarus when he was called from the open grave. Secondly, the recently dead son of the widow of Nain, when he was called from the open coffin, and firstly, the fresh little corpse of Jairus's daughter, when she was called back from the dead in a closed room. We might also note that Christ resurrected the young, the mature and the old, in a closed space, a bustling space and an open space! In a private space, in a public space and in a open space for all the world to see!

It is amply evident that the importunity faith of others and the mere compassion of Christ upon the genuine grieving, seem to have Him move to act out of His timeline.

We could, but we shall not, go into the Kingdom reasons for the timing of the Lord revealing Himself to Israel. Suffice to say, that it seems to me that Christ has His timings, His scheduling, and His planning. There was a time and a place for 'going public.' Even so, it is also amply evident that the importunate faith of others and the mere compassion of Christ upon the genuine grieving of the parents, seem to have Him move to act out of His timeline.

It is said that, 'the life of one human being cannot be used merely as means for another's peace or welfare.' Yet the widows son was raised for her present peace and future welfare, and the daughter of Jairus was raised for the immediate consolation of both the parents. There may have been other unseen reasons but these are the only reasons to be seen and from them we should find great encouragement to pray for our own dead children.

We know what infamous and devilish destruction came from the progeny of the spared Hezekiah. Even so, God knew it and allowed it. We do not know what blessing or cursing could come from the progeny of the daughter of Jairus or the son of the widow of Nain. Even so, God allowed their resurrection..

God can do whatever He likes, however, I believe God will only call back the dead to participate in this life, only if the departed spirits of those dead were if pre-Pentecost, in the bosom of Abraham, and post-Pentecost, in Christ. Despite their tours and book sales, I have my grave doubts about all of hell's so called 2nd chancers.

We do not know the long term consequences of our prayers of faith. How can we? Our prayers, moved more often than not by the deep passion for our own present consolation or the deep compassion for another's, are really all that often move us. We rarely have a future plan in our prayers, yes, we rarely have a future grand design or purpose. We are creatures of the immediate present, seeking consolation in the here and in the now. Therefore, for all our dead children, those spiritually dead, let us pray for their salvation, even for their spiritual resurrection. Their eternal future must be secured. What their temporal future shall be or the future prospect of their progeny, we must leave with God, else we shall go mad! So, we are taught to number our days, and to pray for our daily bread, and that each day has enough trouble of its own and that daily cares are really all we can healthily cope with. Yes, we are presently fitted mostly to be creatures of the present day.

I counsel you in this, that whether the corpse sits up and speaks or not, you must leave their future with God, for a creature of the present day, has no power over future days, nor over the people yet to come.

Let present faith then , and present need, and present desire, and present passion, and present compassion, move you to pray for resurrection. Indeed, may you see the goodness of the Lord in the land of the living. Amen. However, I counsel you in this, that whether the corpse sits up and speaks or not, you must leave their future with God, for a creature of the present day, has no power over future days, nor over the people yet to come.

Listen: *While He was still speaking, someone came from the ruler of the synagogue's house, saying to him, "Your daughter is dead. Do not trouble the Teacher." But when Jesus heard it, He answered him, saying, "Do not be afraid; only believe, and she will be made well." (Luke 8:49-51 NKJV)*

Pray: Lord, look upon us and have pity upon us, Oh great Father, in Christ, because of Christ, through Christ, have compassion upon us we pray. We ask You for our possessed children. Release them O Lord from the devil. We pray for our rebel children O Lord, defeat their wayward heart and bring down their castles of self-destruction. We pray for our sick children, heal them O Lord, amen. We pray for our dead children, raise them O Lord! Raise them from the dead. Father, Lord Jesus, Master, Lord of life and love, place the warm and living hands of our dead daughters and departed sons back into ours we pray, indeed O God, may we see the goodness of the Lord in this, even in the land of our living. Amen and let it be so, yes, amen, and let it be so.

Night-Whisper | **LIFE**

Nehemiah 10:29

and we will not neglect the house of our God.

Force out the Pharisee!

Religion has a momentum all of its own. God may have removed His presence, His blessing and His glory but it makes no difference to religious momentum! The religious committees are elected, entrusted and empowered and they will do their job no matter what. I recently heard of a church of 45 people which had been in decline for over 10 years having problems recruiting folk for the 75 committees it presently had established to run this "vast organization". It is silly isn't it? It really is.

Nehemiah 10:29

and we will not neglect the house of our God.NKJV

Interestingly though, our physical body parallels this problem in that we could have been in decline for years as well and yet we still ill-treat it and live with problems that with just a little attention, a good diet, exercise and minimal medical intervention, we could eliminate and maybe even then go on to improve our health, effectiveness and lifespan. The same accepted and blind decline can also apply to our spiritual bodies and frankly, I find it rather amazing when I contemplate the death we so easily accommodate ourselves to in living within both the physical and spiritual realms. How easily we come to terms with creeping death. This needs to change. You know, restoration of any dilapidated house takes attention, effort, and resources, and no doubt some pain! It is the same with our physical and spiritual houses and especially with respect to our dying local churches.

Now here is a problem for many of our local churches. When in decline and disrepair, the united repentant effort that is required to turn the situation around often calls for resources that our tired, lazy, blind and self-justifying disposition just does not have. The parts of the local body wanting to live know that they now have a fight on their hands, even a civil war! Once this fight for life begins, two things will then undoubtedly happen. Either the religiously diseased parts, eventually die, or for some reason they depart, allowing health to slowly but surely spread. Or secondly, those seeking life will leave the relationship of death. They have to, or they too shall die with the leprous blind and they know it.

Whether outwardly forced by the religiously sick or internally moved by a spiritual survival mechanism, those with life eventually leave these dying churches allowing them a speedier ride on the back of the pale green horse. Such terminal departure might only be stopped when religious committees cease to manage death, or preferably cease to manage! This is very, very rare.

Whether outwardly forced by the religiously sick or internally moved by a spiritual survival mechanism, those with life eventually leave these dying churches!

Let us get on our knees and look to Him who is the administrator of light and life and love. Things can be better. They really can. It's worth the effort! Do you see it? Do you want it? Force out the Pharisee! It is not tolerance and love to let them stay and rule, it is death to the church, it is death to your family, it is death to you!

Listen: *"therefore choose life, that both you and your descendants may live." Deut30:19*

Pray: Lord of life, please forgive for our laziness and love of death and mobilise us to choose life! Amen and amen!

Night-Whisper | **OBEY**

Hearing, heartlands and the state that we are in

It is a solemn and serious privilege to hear the word of God. The church of the recent past sold its soul to simplicity in replacing sermons with talks, and in the so doing, has downgraded the Word of God to mere ideas and suggestions for the careful considerations of the unconcerned. Few were concerned, fewer still considered. The downgrading of the communicating of the word of God, from the solemnity of preaching and the cutting and digging of a sermon, is the main reason for the state we are in.

Luke 8:16-18

"No one, when he has lit a lamp, covers it with a vessel or puts it under a bed, but sets it on a lampstand, that those who enter may see the light. For nothing is secret that will not be revealed, nor anything hidden that will not be known and come to light. Therefore take heed how you hear. For whoever has, to him more will be given; and whoever does not have, even what he seems to have will be taken from him." NKJV

You can wake the sleeper. The non-Christian will be awoken from the dead by the preaching of God's word. He might wake angry, but he will be awoken. The lackadaisical Zombie Christian who is having what seed he had given him, either choked or stolen from him, might also be awakened by the preaching, teaching and proclamation of God's word. These people, like all the new recently roused, awaken into twilight and will expect more light to be given to them.

Remember, a talk can never wake people up. Dead people and sleeping people, need to be roused! This is done by loud ploughing, this is done by the deep cutting of the soil.

The dead, or those asleep, cannot be made concerned. However, twilight people, the rub-eye newly awakened mole people, can now be made concerned by the further preaching, teaching and proclamation of God's word. I have never seen a dead person or a sleeping person show one ounce of concern. But those awakened into the twilight zone, can be made concerned by the preaching, teaching and the proclamation of God's word. This is tilling, this is the removing of rocks and stones.

Once the surface of the heartland is prepared, you can then arouse the spiritual interests of those now made concerned for their own soul and their own spiritual well-being. Here, what ground of the heart is presented, may now be sown into. Yes, the good seed can now be sown. Look now, for the presented ground which the seed is sowed into is not yours to choose, but rather, it is what is presented to you by 'the awakened concerned.' Oh, for sure, as a faithful husbandman, as a faithful Pastor, you may very well continue to water the seed of God's word and bring Sonlight to it, but the great difference between the soil of this earth and the heart of a man, is that the heart of a man now takes great responsibility for itself. The soil of the earth cannot do this, but the heart of a man can do this and is required to do this. We can say, maybe, that the heart is land which chooses what kind of soil it is, and what kind of place the soil shall manifest itself in. For example, shall the soil be in a shallow place? Shall the heart soil be amongst the rock or amongst the weeds? Look now, for the presenting and placing of the soil is down to the choice of the awakened and concerned. Listen now, for the awakened and concerned heartland of a man is malleable, and it is shapeable, both by the Preachers ploughing and tilling and by its own care, attention and choosing.

> *Look now, for the presented ground which the seed is sowed into is not yours to choose, but rather, it is what is presented to you by 'the awakend concerned.'*

The Word has been preached, the dead and sleeping have been awakened into twilight, further preaching has opened up the heartland of their being and they have been made concerned for their state, and the sower sent to sow has now sewn the Divine seed of His Word into the ground presented to him and it has been further fed and watered. HOWEVER, It is now the job of the heartlands of an awaked and concerned, sewn and well-watered man to now **TAKE HEED HOW THEY LISTEN!!** The soil now takes full responsibility for itself, for something of inestimable value, has been given and this can be taken away or choked and diminished. **Therefore, be careful how you listen, take heed how you hear.** Is the Divine seed weak? NO! It is a seed, and it is the responsibility of the heartland to move it from the surface to the depths of our being. I say again, the grade of heartland soil, its depth and positioning is dependent upon how we hear the word of God. Remember that it is a solemn and serious privilege to hear the Word of God. The church of the recent past sold its soul to simplicity in replacing sermons with talks, and in the so doing, has downgraded the Word of God to mere ideas and suggestions for the careful considerations of the unconcerned.

The Question is this, "How do the awakened and concerned increase the openness, position depth and quality of their soil?" The answer is simple, by obeying that which they have already heard. Action, obedience, implementation, DOING the Word of God is the only thing that affects the heartland for good. Auditing the Word of God, meditating on it, memorizing it, knowing it, is all well and good, but it is as useful as an ash tray on a motorbike or a chocolate fireguard if it is not applied by action. **Be doers of the word and not hearers only**!

Let us who are alive, DO the word of God. Today, tomorrow and everyday thereafter then, walk in the light by doing the light, and so let your abundance be seen by all.

'Doing' the word of God will bless and transform you. Then, not only will the seed both flower and fruit, but to those who have much, more will be given, for all fruit contains seeds!

The danger of NOT doing is also made clear. Even that which he has been given to him shall be taken away from him! Hard heartlands lead to barrenness, and barrenness leads to desert badlands.

It has been suggested that the root problems with the church now nearly gone, has not been its lack of orthodoxy but rather its lack of orthopraxy, that is, it's not DOING the Word. The flip side of this observation is that lack of orthopraxy will lead to heresy. Let us therefore who are alive, DO the word of God. Today, tomorrow and everyday thereafter then, walk in the light by DOING the light, and so let your abundance be seen by all.

Listen: *Then His mother and brothers came to Him, and could not approach Him because of the crowd. And it was told Him by some, who said, "Your mother and Your brothers are standing outside, desiring to see You." But He answered and said to them, "My mother and My brothers are these who hear the word of God and do it." (Luke 8:19-21 NKJV)*

Pray: Father, in this matter, I have greatly failed. Lord Jesus, light of the world light of everyman that comes into the world, shine on me once again for I choose to obey and do Your word. Test me in this. God the Holy Spirit, aid me in this, empower me in this, provoke me in this, annoy me in this, cajole me in this, rightly comfort me in this my desire to do Thy will O God. Amen and let it be so.

Night-Whisper | **FIGHT**

Mi-nute men or minitmen!

S ome people have said it was Longfellow's poem that made Paul Revere and his ride an important event in American History.

Isaiah 40:9

"O Zion, You who bring good tidings, Get up into the high mountain; O Jerusalem, You who bring good tidings, lift up your voice with strength, lift it up, be not afraid; say to the cities of Judah, "Behold your God!" NKJV

Listen my children and you shall hear
Of the midnight ride of Paul Revere,
On the eighteenth of April
, in Seventy-five;
Hardly a man is now alive
Who remembers that famous
day and year.

The contents of the poem, the facts of the ride, the man himself, and even the supposed cry of "The British are coming," have all been subjects of historical dispute. Even so, these facts remain true:

People were aware of the times.

People were watching and waiting.

People were ready at a minutes notice to bear arms and fight for what they thought was right!

Friends, where are the watchers and the minute men of the church today? Where are the prophets and the proclaimers, the true disciples and disdainers of all that glitters and is not gold. Where are the spiritual fighters and the holy men of old?

Our enemies are not primarily flesh and blood but our warfare is mostly and primarily spiritual. So, where are the spiritual fighting men of this our day, where are the warrior women? When looking back at our time to put a stamp of victory on the pages of His story, who will call these days and years famous? Who will seek to remember them, or maybe rather seek not to remember them for fear of shame and embarrassment as the stamp of victory has had to be replaced with the smudge of defeat.

The words of another American, William P Merril, maybe should be sung at the multitude of leadership, family and marriage conferences that teach men how to be nice and to get along, maybe this should be the old new song that shakes the salt cellar of the church so much, that the damp and lumpy masculine mess which it now is, begins to come apart a little?

Rise up, O men of God!
The church for you doth wait,
Her strength unequal to her task;
Rise up and make her great!

Lift high the cross of Christ!
Tread where His feet have trod.
As brothers of the Son of Man,
Rise up, O men of God

Listen: *Another popular lyric poem from long ago reads like this: "Then the horses hooves pounded, The galloping, galloping of his steeds. 'Curse Meroz,' said the angel of the LORD, 'Curse its inhabitants bitterly, Because they did not come to the help of the LORD, to the help of the LORD against the mighty.'" Judges 5:22,23*

Pray: Lord, awaken me, heal me, help me, arm me, that I may be mentioned in eternal dispatches and known on the field of battle. O my God do not let my carelessness become my curse. In me, I ask it O Lord, in me I say, "Rise up O Lord, O Lord our God may Your enemies all be scattered!" Lord, come shake my damp old saltcellar, shake it Lord, shake it hard over the pages of my history!

Night-Whisper | **AUTHENTIC**

Are we just morons with a message?

I remember when the tall young Southern preacher touched on the text above. It was so good it needs repeating. Apparently, the Greek word for "losing flavor" is from where we get our English word, "moron".

Matthew 5:13

"You are the salt of the earth; but if the salt loses its flavor, how shall it be seasoned? It is then good for nothing but to be thrown out and trampled underfoot by men." NKJV

The word means insipid, stupid, dull, dumb, and moronic! And you know friends, when the church loses its saltiness, that's just how she appears to the world. Moronic! Jesus seems to intimate, that there is no solution to this problem at all! When the salt has become good for nothing; once the flavor has gone, what can you do but throw it out?

We imagine loss of flavor to be due primarily to some severe moral transgression, or especially maybe, to some doctrinal heresy. For sure, either of these can be catastrophic for the church and I am afraid to say, both are increasingly common. However, I'm not sure that's what Jesus meant? There's something far more endemic here which we have to deal with, for doctrinal dispute means nothing to the world, they are not interested and frankly, moral failure comes as no surprise to them as they are often more honest about their sins and failures than most Christians are of theirs! Don't misunderstand me here; I am not downplaying the wrongness and impact of either problem, I just think there is something worse, some might say far, far worse. For when the world tastes us, it finds us unbelievably, bland! Luke warm blandness is the present curse of the Laodicean church.

A flavorless church is a church which is like a body without nerves, without feeling, without passion, without expression and therefore, it is a church without a present voice, her own distinct, clear as crystal voice, all colored like a pomegranate, fragrant as freesias warmed by the sun on the kitchen windowsill, smelt on a late Friday afternoon, as unforgettable as Dutch liquorice and Cuban coffee.

This bland voiceless kind of church however, as inoffensive as a well-dressed toddler, can only offer lessons in politeness, diplomas in acceptance and degrees in mediocrity. This moronic, flavorless, voiceless church is above all, respectable. This moronic church though, appears to have it all together and the members of this church are neat, clean cut, financially viable, and have all their teeth smilingly enameled. If they have a story, it is encased in the past

> *This moronic, flavorless, voiceless church is above all, respectable.*

tense. They certainly have no struggles now. Have no victories, have no weeping defeats, have no joy of journey, no, they are in every understanding of the word, senseless and so are subsequently, voiceless, bland and tasteless!

The world however, has stories in the present tense, and struggles of every kind. It's taste buds are primed and dancing. So, when the world dares to taste this kind of voiceless church it finds it bland, as expected. When it looks with investigation, it finds it featureless, when it listens it finds it to be but clanging cymbals, full of a people so irrelevant to them and to what they need, that these poor voiceless but *all together churches* appear to the watching world as just a bunch of morons with a message and a less than mediocre message at that!

What's your church like today? Full of *five-flavor lifesavers* or just neatly packaged boxes of doctrinally correct, dried up oatmeal that is good for nothing except to be thrown out? What's your church like today? Full of *five-flavor lifesavers* or just frothy unfermented new wine. All smulched up with silly love songs that are good for nothing except to be thrown out? If it is either of these, then I have no word of encouragement for you, except that you get out before the housewife of the Holy Spirit throws you out of the window and into the street to be trampled underfoot. He, who has ears to hear, let him hear!

Listen: *"Go out quickly into the streets and lanes of the city, and bring in here the poor and the maimed and the lame and the blind." Then the master said to the servant, "Go out into the highways and hedges, and compel them to come in, that my house may be filled. For I say to you that none of those men who were invited shall taste my supper." Luke 14:21-24*

Pray: Real God, in all my troubles, really be seen in me today! When I am touched and tasted, may I be found full of Your goodness, yes, let me at least rejoice in the knowledge that the flavor of Christ my Savior is found in all my troubles, in Jesus name I pray, Amen.

Touching toads

A man walks into a psychiatrist's office and says that he thinks he's a toad. Looking sympathetically the doctor says, "Well hop onto the couch. I want you to tell me every little detail about yourself, warts and all!"

1 Corinthians 4:5

Therefore judge nothing before the time, until the Lord comes, who will both bring to light the hidden things of darkness and reveal the counsels of the hearts. NKJV

It's an old joke but I like it. The saying "warts and all" is attributed to the leader of the only republic England ever had, Oliver Cromwell. Speaking to his French portrait painter Mr. Peter Lily, Cromwell is reputed to have said *"I desire you would use all your skill to paint my picture truly like me, and not flatter me at all; but remark all these roughnesses, pimples, warts and all; otherwise I never will pay a farthing for it."* Cromwell of course had an enormous wart on his face. It seems to me this man at the very least, was a brave realist.

It's true that when we are brave enough, we all long for realism. Until that is, we begin to see the picture that is painted for us! When the warts are revealed for us for all the world to see, our courage often exchanges places with self-justifying cowardice! When this happens to us and my friends please be assured that it eventually happens to us all, we need to find some solitude for our revealed ugliness, to then begin to seek the all-seeing God.

Prayer I think, is like being in the psychiatrist chair. We get a chance to speak with Jesus and tell Him how we feel, what we truly think, warts and all. It's an enormous release to be able to go to God and just speak about the real things that are pressing in on us, bending us almost to breaking point. Here in prayer, we get the opportunity to be relieved of our burdens, to find counsel, solace, and comfort in our most ugly time of need. Yes, our most ugliest time of need. "Don't hide anything, just come" says Jesus. "Cast all your care on me for I care greatly for you."

Prayer however, is a two way process, and Jesus speaks as well. When we are ready, and sometimes I wonder, when He can stand His silence no more, He speaks to us, giving us a true and real diagnosis of our condition. It's often less than flattering, and we often don't like it, but it is the gracious truth, warts and all. I wonder if we are never as good as we think we are, and often far worse than we believe ourselves to be? Are we ready to have such beautiful but grotesque views of ourselves ground into dust, I wonder? Are we ready to listen to Him today?

Jesus speaks as well. When we are ready, and sometimes I wonder, when He can stand His silence no more, He speaks to us, giving us a true and real diagnosis of our condition. It's often less than flattering, and we often don't like it.

Maybe God wants to have a little word with you today about your warts? If so, then don't worry. He is good.

Listen: *"And behold, a leper came and worshiped Him, saying, 'Lord, if You are willing, You can make me clean.' Then Jesus put out His hand and touched him, saying, 'I am willing; be cleansed.' Immediately his leprosy was cleansed." (Matthew 8:2-3)*

Pray: When You reveal my true self to me today O Lord my God, reveal also Your Son in me. Lord, if You are willing, despite my many warts, You can make me clean. Please do it, amen.

Night-Whisper | **PERSEVERANCE**

Even aces make mistakes

The end of the war was only months off by this time and the German air command faced both ever-improving British airplanes and their own dwindling numbers. The German forces now held fewer aces in their hand. Manfred von Richthofen, alias the Red Baron, was shot down today in 1918.

2 Peter 3:16

...as also in all his epistles, speaking in them of these things, in which are some things hard to understand, which untaught and unstable people twist to their own destruction, as they do also the rest of the Scriptures. NKJV

The thrill of the hunt was all but gone for Baron von Richthofen as most of his peers had already been killed and his own wounds agonized him. Though the German air doctrine he himself wrote, stated that, "One should never obstinately stay with an opponent which, through bad shooting or skillful turning, he has been unable to shoot down while the battle lasts, until it is far on the enemy side," he nonetheless chased his British quarry far deeper into enemy territory and far lower to the ground, than his own common sense should have permitted.

British pilot officer May later said that it was only his erratic and untrained piloting which saved him from Richthofen who followed the erratic path of this novice pilot, until a single bullet, shot from behind him, passed diagonally through his chest. Richthofen crashed and burned. After an astonishing 80 kills himself, he was dispatched by a single bullet, either from a gunner on the ground or a chasing Canadian pilot coming to the British pilot's aid. A single bullet and the brightly colored red tri-plane of the Red Baron disappeared forever. Not following his own doctrine led ultimately to his own destruction. Remember that.

As a side note, you might be interested to know that the new commander of Richthofen's squadron chose to paint his plane completely white. A good color you would think to replace the flamboyant and flaunting red of the dead fighter ace? The new commander's name was

Hermann Göring, a most infamous Nazi who would rise to be head of the Luftwaffe. At the Nuremburg trials, he poisoned himself the night before his execution for crimes against humanity.

Listen: *"You therefore, beloved, since you know this beforehand, beware lest you also fall from your own steadfastness, being led away with the error of the wicked;" 2 Peter 3:17*

Pray: Lord, help me to hold fast my confession without wavering. The day is long, and I am tired. Come to my aid O Lord my God. Amen.

Night-Whisper | **TRUST**

Filthy love

Fagin's philosophy sounds so very true. "In this life one thing counts, in the bank, large amounts!" After all, if you are unhappy with your face or body? Money will fix it. Do you need a place to live? Money will fix it. Do you need transportation, debt alleviation, a large building for a growing congregation, need to pacify a small roguish nation or buy a nice cut jewel for her celebration? Well money will fix it, 'cause money fixes most things friends! Oh yes it does!

1 John 2:17

And the world is passing away, and the lust of it.
NKJV

We all know it's money that makes this world go around and not love. Prestige, respect, safeties of all sorts in the many forms of medical insurance and life insurance and retirement benefits and well, you name it; are all provided by money! So get money and remember, if you're overflowing with all that lovely green stuff and don't know what to do with it, then may I quote Fagin once more? "Robin Hood, what a crook! Gave away, what he took. Charity's fine, subscribe to mine."

Actually, money is great; it brings a certain freedom with it. Ask any arts group and they shall tell you how money from patrons and sponsors release them to perform. After all, without philanthropic patrons the rest of the country would not be able to get to the stock exchange for falling over starving artists dying in droves on all the pavements and sidewalks of our cities! Ah money, don't you just love it? Such a key to the opening of locked doors, such freedom, such supply, such happiness that comes with having money. I like the look of lucre, don't you? Of course you do. Money does have a strange power doesn't it? For though I have God living in my heart, yet I know that I am a different man, a better man, more at peace and more assured, when I have a few hundred dollars in my back pocket and you know, that concerns me greatly, for oh, the peace that money brings me and oh the plastic pompousness that comes from having some money in my own back pocket! Even the power of His

Golden presence seems to be enhanced when couched in green. Scary stuff! Spiritually speaking, maybe we would be better off without it?

There is however, no Godliness in poverty just as there is no evil in riches.

There is however, no Godliness in poverty just as there is no evil in riches. However, let's face it, the seeming freedom and safety and open doors and the power that money brings with it, does give money an exceptionally strong magnetic pull. Who hasn't felt it? Yet as gravity warps light, so the love of money and the attractive danger of that kind of fiscal freedom, that kind of financial fortressing of our earthly futures, both distorts our view of eternity and bends us away from trust in the Father. On many occasions, Jesus saw money's binding power on those possessed by it and His loving direction to those imprisoned by their wealth or desire for it was simple, "Give it up, give it away!"

In such demanding proclamation, in both pictures of camels and eyes of needles, it seems to me that Jesus showed us not only the giant bastion of unbelief but also the all-possessing fortress of great possessions. Tell me friends, how many green humps are you riding on today?

Listen: *"For the love of money is a root of all kinds of evil, for which some have strayed from the faith in their greediness, and pierced themselves through with many sorrows." 1 Timothy 6:9-10*

Pray: Oh my Father, I am tempted not to trust in You and in Your goodness. In the building of my wooden barns, the laying down of the hay my future and the storing up of all my stubble, I fear I am but building for myself simply a big and burning bonfire to warm my hands on both now and in my latter days. Please forgive me O Lord, and help me to put my hope in You for Oh my Father, I am tempted not to trust in You and in Your goodness towards me, Your little child. Amen!

Night-Whisper | **CONSIDER**

Wonky at work

My wife had made some cakes, which had filled the house with that homely sweet smell that made you hungry and happy all at the same time! I was there when she bought the mixture that she intended to bake at school for some of the young ones she was taking care of, so why was she cooking them here? For me? "Oh," she says, "I couldn't cook them for the kids yesterday because the oven was 'wonky' at work." That made me smile! Of course, you all know what you call a three-legged donkey? A wonkey!

Romans 5:3

And not only that, but we also glory in tribulations.
NKJV

It's a funny old thing that being like Christ in our present Christian culture is translated as being, "as near perfect as you possibly can be." If you are a leader or even if you're simply, "mature in the faith," then you are definitely not allowed to have problems. If you do, then please keep them to yourself, thank you very much!

I can understand the often heard but rarely seen, frantic brush of broken pieces under the carpet, for the church has had some terrible examples of leadership and the world has rightly laughed us to scorn. Such bad leadership has embarrassed Jesus and put Him to open shame. However, my proposition is this: We have the tendency to set ourselves up for a fall, for who after all, is sufficient to rightly represent Jesus in His perfections by being perfect in themselves? Maybe it might do us all a lot of good to remember that we are all a little, wonky at work.

Jesus has a cunning plan in enticing sinners to His love and grace. He takes His glory, His forgiveness, His very presence and places them in pots of clay. That's us folks, just pots of clay and the truth about us, is that we are all cracked pots! These flaws, these cracks of various dimensions depth and proportion are there in each one of us, so let's just face it, because it's just farcical to hide it. We are all cracked pots. The wonder of this though, is that the Glory of Christ Himself, shines out of the cracks! Could there be anything more enticing to other cracked pots but to see shining glory pouring out of the flaws of other but redeemed cracked pots?

Imagine today being approached by a fellow Christian who asks, "Hey how are you?" If you replied, "Well I'm feeling hard pressed, perplexed, persecuted, and struck down." I am pretty sure you would enter into some diagnostic discourse that would lead to pastoral counsel, after all,

We are all cracked pots. The wonder of this though, is that the Glory of Christ Himself, shines out of the cracks!

you'd be concerned about your fellow believer wouldn't you? However, maybe we shouldn't be, maybe we should just shout "glory!" and even "glory hallelujah!" After all, maybe we are all a little wonky at work for a Divine purpose? Yes, Paul's personal testimony is most instructive.

Listen: *"Because of the extravagance of those revelations, and so I wouldn't get a big head, I was given the gift of a handicap to keep me in constant touch with my limitations. Satan's angel did his best to get me down; what he in fact did was push me to my knees. No danger then of walking around high and mighty! At first I didn't think of it as a gift, and begged God to remove it. Three times I did that, and then he told me, My grace is enough; it's all you need. My strength comes into its own in your weakness. Once I heard that, I was glad to let it happen. I quit focusing on the handicap and began appreciating the gift. It was a case of Christ's strength moving in on my weakness. Now I take limitations in stride, and with good cheer, these limitations that cut me down to size — abuse, accidents, opposition, bad breaks. I just let Christ take over! And so the weaker I get, the stronger I become." (From The Message: The Bible in Contemporary Language © 2002 by Eugene H. Peterson. 2 Corinthians 12:7-10)*

Pray: Father, let me not settle in my sin but never the less be able to glory in Your gigantic grace toward me in Jesus Christ the Lord of cracked pots, amen and amen!

Night-Whisper | **CONSIDER**

A simple summary of all forms and formats

T he very first books purchased for the American Library of Congress were from London. $5,000 of available funds were used to buy a collection of 740 volumes and just three maps. Today, over 200 years since its foundation, the vast holdings of the library now number well over 110 million items and continues to grow daily.

Ecclesiastes 12:12

Of making many books there is no end, and much study is wearisome to the flesh. NKJV

Being around for just a little longer of course, the British Library has over 150 million items and reports that 3 million items are added to its shelves annually, their shelves increasing in length by 12km per year. Now that's amazing! Someone has estimated that if you were to attempt to read a book a day in the British library and from its existing inventory only mind you, that it would take you well over 400,000 years to get through them!

With the arrival of the digital era and the now widespread self-publishing it has brought with it, the increase of books in every form and format is frankly even now, enormous! Indeed, the making of so many books is now so prolific that I wonder if soon and very soon, we are going to be living in the library!

In this busy age we live in, with easy access to this vast amount of information, it's important to have a service that picks out the best of the best and neatly summarizes them for us. These very useful services are growing each day. In this regard however, once again, may I say that God was way ahead of everyone else!

You see, many centuries ago God employed a researcher and supplied him with all the resources necessary both materially, intellectually and spiritually to investigate the meaning of life and the purpose of the existence of humanity, living under this hot and not so happy sun. Solomon's years of investigation and experimentation proved a useful journal of instruction and explanation, and thank God, just for us busy people, Solomon provided us with a summary of his findings, the best and most accurate of all the available information. Here it is:

Listen: *"Let us hear the conclusion of the whole matter: Fear God and keep His commandments, for this is man's all. For God will bring every work into judgment, including every secret thing, whether good or evil."* *Ecclesiastes 12:13-14*

Pray: Lord, help me to live rightly, daily, nightly, in the whole conclusion of this great matter. Help me to fear You and keep all Your commandments, in Jesus name I pray, amen.

Night-Whisper | **PRAY**

Fighting talk

L ittle if nothing is archeologically known of the Amalekites today. However, the Bible tells us that these are the people who blocked the path of the escaping Israelites from the tyranny of Pharaoh when they were going to the promised land; these are the people who attacked the stragglers, the tired and the weary on their way to the Holy Land; these are the people who hindered and hardened the way into the land flowing with milk and honey. It's not unreasonable then, to view the Amalekites as a symbol for every evil and hatred against the redemption of God's people. Maybe we need to remember that? Indeed, God says in **Deuteronomy 25:19, "Remember the Amalekites, blot them out of history, and don't forget what they did to you."** I tell you, in this same Deuteronomic destructive way, we too must remember the Amalekites!

Exodus 17:12,13

Aaron and Hur supported his hands, one on one side, and the other on the other side; and his hands were steady until the going down of the sun. So Joshua defeated Amalek and his people with the edge of the sword. NKJV

Any person or group of people journeying towards Zion, journeying towards all the promises of God which are "yes and let it be done" in Christ Jesus, well it is these people who are on the Highway of Holiness and journeying towards God's promised land. Let it be known today then, that on this highway, you shall meet the fiercest of foes, even the destroyer himself. More than anything though you shall meet the raiding, restricting and resentful Amalekites.

Now friends this is where we have to get real. Holiness and the pursuance of God and His promises, God and His city, God and His land, does not mean the presence of peace! Au contraire mes amies, it means the most definite practice of war! Following hard after God you see, causes a disturbance in the heavenlies. Did you not know that such marching disturbances, even such miniscule movement towards the practice of holiness and the power of spiritual authority is like a giant blip on the enemy's radar and causes them to come screaming and screeching to check you out and even chuck you out! Didn't you know that when the enemy loses ground to you, he counter attacks? Didn't you know that when the enemy loses people from his kingdom, he terrorizes those involved in the rescue? Meditative, smirking, monastic montages of true Christianity do not need armor my friends but true walkers of the Way will need it on them, every single day, I say, every single day! Get real for goodness sake! Go, get tooled up!

The powerful weapon of choice to be used against the Amalekites is that of "all prayer". This "broad sword" of "all prayer" is tiring to use, especially when the battle is long, even all the day and our hearts get weary watching the advance and retreat of battle, waiting and watching, looking and longing for the final breakthrough. Even mighty Moses would not have prevailed in prayer

Meditative, smirking, monastic montages of true Christianity do not need armor my friends but true walkers of the Way will need it on them, every single day, I say, every single day!

without the help of Aaron and Hur, both at his right and at his left, lifting up his hands and I tell you, it is the same with you. Wielding the weapon of all prayer is very hard indeed! Get help now.

Are the Amalekites on you today? Then you must shout for help! Sound the alarm, ring the number, send the prayer letter, get the friends, bang out that email, beg the prayers, and get the people of God around you lifting you up, so that you can fight in prayer, after all that is what prayer is isn't it? Fighting talk?

Listen: *"...praying always with all prayer and supplication in the Spirit, being watchful to this end with all perseverance and supplication for all the saints" Ephesians 6:18*

Pray: HELP LORD! Send I pray, help from Your throne! Amen and amen!

Night-Whisper | **FRIENDSHIP**

Acquiring The Accent

Not so very long ago, in the United Kingdom of Great Britain and Northern Ireland, if one wanted to get on in broadcasting, then one had to speak the Queen's English in a very proper polite and monotone kind of way, don't you know. Indeed, once upon a time speaking this way seemed to be the only real sign of good breeding and good schooling. "Jolly good, old chap!" Now of course, the more of a regional accent you have the more you might be heard! Regional accents today have "street cred" you see, because it's seemingly more authentic; less pompous, more PC don't you know. My, how times have changed. "Rather!"

Acts 4:13

Now when they saw the boldness of Peter and John, and perceived that they were uneducated and untrained men, they marvelled. NKJV

My own origins in the Midlands of the United Kingdom, make my accent very regional indeed, even common; that is in the lower, poorer, less educated understanding of the word "common" of course. You can imagine then how wonderful it is for such a commoner to have lived in the South of the USA and find it hilarious, that the accent of such a commoner is regarded there with real enchantment, endearment and appreciation. If only they knew!

The early apostles were perceived, that is seen to be, uneducated and untrained men. I want to suggest to you it was because they were Galileans and you could hear it in their voice, in their accent and after all that's said and done, everyone knew that *"nothing good ever came from Galilee!"* These poor uneducated men that looked the part, walked the part and sounded the part of goofy Galileans did on the surface, seem to be living proof of that very same discriminating saying! Yet these regional renegades caused the authorities to marvel, even to be astonished in wonderful admiration at how they handled themselves and spoke with such authority. It would appear that these Galilean scum, had acquired a new and overriding spiritual accent. Thankfully it is a new and universal over riding accent and all who hear it, give testimony to its power, its loveliness, its veracity and its desirability and like so many accents, it is best acquired by spending a lot of time around the person speaking it.

Friend, just who are you spending most of your time with? It's going to tell in the way you speak don't you know? "Rather!"

Listen: *"...they marvelled. And they realized that they had been with Jesus." Acts 4:13-14*

Pray: O Lord, open my lips, and my mouth shall show forth Your praise. (Psalms51:15)

-Whisper | **ACTION**

Black Sky Days

Jeremiah's book of lamentations recounts the punishments of the iniquity of the daughter of God's people, even the dear people of the Lord, whose punishment turned out to be greater than that of Sodom! No wonder Jeremiah wept so much. He was overcome with the visions of the Lord and also from being part of the beginnings of their actual fulfillment. I cannot help but see some parallels as to his prayer in our text this evening, my spirit saying along with him, "Remember, O Lord, what has come upon us; Look, and behold our reproach!"

Lamentations 5:1-4

Remember, O Lord, what has come upon us; Look, and behold our reproach! Our inheritance has been turned over to aliens, And our houses to foreigners. We have become orphans and waifs, Our mothers are like widows. We pay for the water we drink, And our wood comes at a price. NKJV

The inheritance of the now slain giant Albion left to its sons and daughters has in the past been mostly its culture, especially as expressed in its architecture, institutions, education, dress, manners and language. Everything to do with Western culture has essentially been touched and shaped by Biblical Christianity. No more and not for a good while now.

'Black Sky Days' are a term used by electric infrastructure security experts when discussing, in particular, a collapse of the North American power grid. The enormous concern of those planners is not of the cost of repairing such an outage, or even its impact on the financial block and production block of the nation, but rather, on the virtually and immediate collapse of society which would occur shortly after. 'Black Sky Days' indeed!

In the past, Biblical principles and the presence of the Holy Spirit held society together when the sun went down. Listen now, when the fullness of the real Black Sky Days come upon us, I wonder if so very quickly we shall be plunged into darker days than Jeremiah ever had nightmares of and that right quickly.

Meanwhile, as the light of Christianity flickers out in the West, consider our text for this evening. Look now, our inheritance has been handed over to aliens and our houses to foreigners. It is pointless quoting the

Look now, our inheritance has been handed over to aliens and our houses to foreigners.

figures of foreign investment and occupancy in Britain, they are freely available for your own research and will shock you. In many Britain's major cities, including its capital, its indigenous people are increasingly in the minority, and while the overall Muslim population is currently around 3-4% they are making the most noise and are making the most changes. This will increase. Islamic banking and financing is growing 50% faster than traditional banking in Britain and the financial portfolio and an examination of the influence of such financing on key British education centers you will find to be both impressive and powerful. Our inheritance has been turned over to aliens and our houses to foreigners.

Government figures say that last night over 100,000 British children went to sleep homeless. Uncounted other 'sofa-surfers' sleep their nights away in other peoples rented properties and fritter away their days on nonsense. The rise of the single multiple mom is catastrophic and so much so, that the rise of the fatherless 'Orphan,' and the effects of the same is a national disgrace and debilitation. Indeed, there are many mothers who are widowed by absentee fathers. Some of them are widowed many times!

Without looking at the fact that we pay an horrendous price for that which falls daily from our skies in these islands, indeed, we are so disgusted by government fluoridation of the water and who knows what else, that we also pay through the nose for plastic bottles full of untouched spring water, and to top it all, even today, I shall engage in another telephone war with a foreigner to get them to bring down the cost of my direct debit for gas and electricity, which they have, without consultation, decided to hike and take out of my account. Our wood comes at a price and an increasing one at that. Living in the West is coming at the price of utter financial bondage, and many can't even afford the price of becoming a slave to the system.

In the end, despite the numerous confluences of all our greedy and selfish streams, this polluted river, is the judgement of the Lord, and it is soon to burst its banks and break down all our walls. Christian, are you ready and prepared for what's to come for I fear there is no turning back the swelling of this river.

New Antiochs, even cities of Christian strength which must rise up in the west and be populated by end-time disciples.

I pray again for the raising up of end-time Patriarchs to lead the people of God into New Antiochs, even cities of Christian strength which must rise up in the west and be populated by end-time disciples. These cities of light and brotherly love must be populated by the Gypsy Rechabites of the Lord, for a time, times and half time, so that light can be gathered and then sent out to the nations once more.

To get ready for the coming 'Black Sky Days,' you need to prepare to relocate and plan to meet and overcome the coming cumulus gloom.

Listen: *Now when He had taken the scroll, the four living creatures and the twenty-four elders fell down before the Lamb, each having a harp, and golden bowls full of incense, which are the prayers of the saints. And they sang a new song, saying: "You are worthy to take the scroll, And to open its seals; For You were slain, And have redeemed us to God by Your blood Out of every tribe and tongue and people and nation, And have made us kings and priests to our God; And we shall reign on the earth." Then I looked, and I heard the voice of many angels around the throne, the living creatures, and the elders; and the number of them was ten thousand times ten thousand, and thousands of thousands, saying with a loud voice: "Worthy is the Lamb who was slain To receive power and riches and wisdom, And strength and honor and glory and blessing!" And every creature which is in heaven and on the earth and under the earth and such as are in the sea, and all that are in them, I heard saying: "Blessing and honor and glory and power Be to Him who sits on the throne, And to the Lamb, forever and ever!" Then the four living creatures said, "Amen!" And the twenty-four elders fell down and worshiped Him who lives forever and ever. (Revelation 5:8-14 NKJV)*

Pray: Father, our Great God who calls something out of nothing, raise up for us some new Moses, some new Peter, some new Paul, to lead us all into spiritual strength, mutual sustenance and the renewed holy mission of the Gospel. In Jesus name we ask it, amen and amen.

Touching God

Researchers say that in Asia the growing popularity of communications technologies is providing a way for many people to express their faith? From the daily deliveries of lunar almanacs, to electronic reminders telling you it's time to pray as well as which direction to face when doing so, it's obvious that religion, social relationships and science, are all fitting together quite nicely in the technology of the 21st Century. Indeed, if you were to go to the website of the Hindu temple of Kentucky, then you would be able to participate in virtual Poojah. Just click on the screen, connect to your chosen deity and up pops its image (even musically animated) and away you go, twisting on that old jar of poo! Just bow down to your screen, burn your incense and offer up that bunch of bananas in your worship of prayer and sacrifice.

Matthew 9:21

"If only I may touch His garment, I shall be made well." NKJV

Nice and sincere people welcomed me into that same temple, when I was investigating the Hindu religion of some 300 million Gods. I assume, that only the top ranking deities were there that particular morning in Kentucky, as over each shrine, in Arial bold type, were some very specific instructions:

DO NOT TOUCH THE DEITIES

It would appear in most religions that top ranking deities can never be touched! There was no indication about what the temporal or eternal consequences would be if I reached out and clasped the man-made image perched on its shelf in Kentucky, but the command was loud and clear, "Hands off!"

I remember as a young Catholic, in innocent fun reaching into my mouth and pretending to touch the host after my first communion. Older kids who saw me do it, blackmailed me for quite a few weeks after that, forcing me to give them both candy and money, saying they would tell on me for touching God if I didn't meet their demands. Oh no! Now of course, I wouldn't dream of touching any of these particular Hindu deities, it's a dangerous game touching a God! Good grief even the Uzza incident in 1 Chronicles 13 leaves me shocked and fearful every time I read it. If touching wafers and picking at painted plaster can get you into so much trouble, then who of us can reach out, even in dire desperation, reach out and actually touch God and not be killed with His holy and righteous indignation?

God is at your elbow friends, reach out and find Him there! Reach out and touch Him!

Well the magnificent truth for us all today is, that any of us can now in fact reach out and touch God! After all, God clothed Himself in flesh, and we all know that flesh is for touching. Neither technology nor religion must become a veil of fear between us and the living God. Our God touches and can be touched and every trembling finger of faith that lays hold of Jesus, is most richly rewarded. God is at your elbow friends, reach out and find Him there! Reach out and touch Him!

Listen: *"And after eight days His disciples were again inside, and Thomas with them. Jesus came, the doors being shut, and stood in the midst, and said, 'Peace to you!' Then He said to Thomas, 'Reach your finger here, and look at My hands; and reach your hand here, and put it into My side. Do not be unbelieving, but believing.' And Thomas answered and said to Him, 'My Lord and my God!'" John 20:26-28*

"'Be of good cheer, daughter; your faith has made you well.' And the woman was made well from that hour." Matt 9:22

Pray: From the dust O God, my reaching hand trembles at Your lovely feet. Forgiving Father, feel my feeble faith and touch me in return, in Jesus name I ask it, amen!

Night-Whisper | **REMEMBER**

Kindergarten Cop

My wife was once taking care of 20 young people of 4 years of age. In the evening, sometimes when she arrived home with that glazed look in her eyes, I was prompted to ask, "And how were the little angels today?" It's a tin opener type of question and the smell of the answers informed me of just how the next hour or so might play out, whilst the baggage of the day was discarded. Usually I found this question lead to three responses.

Isaiah 1:2

"I have nourished and brought up children, And they have rebelled against Me." NKJV

Response No1: "They were horrible!" This meant they were whiney, noisy, and naughty. The solution; two hot cups of tea and 30 minutes sat in front of "Judge Judy," just to assure her that yes indeed, there are people in the world far more crazier than she feels she is at the moment.

Response No2: "Awful!" Meaning she had a headache, was longing for the weekend and wanted to sleep right now! The solution; three hot cups of tea, two Ibuprofen and chocolate, all to be applied immediately. Holding hands and being hugged profusely to follow.

Response No3: Silence and shaking head. This meant they were demonic! She had already written her resignation letter and all firearms needed to be hidden. No amount of tea, sugar, pills, or "Judge Judy" would justify the insane decision of taking care of 20 children 7 hours a day for pitiful wages. Vasectomy was to be discussed in any future pre-marital counseling I may be giving. It was time for me to leave the building.

Just like us, we have found that children carry sin. It is a constant effort to teach them to do good and to pray for them in the face of their consistent rebellion, that they would choose life and love. It's hard being a parent for when our children do not respond to our loving and careful pleadings and prayers, the self-condemnation we face can be crushing, the unspoken suspicion from other parents can be cutting and the absence of good results from applied Biblical principles can be confusing. However, to my fellow and often troubled parents, will you hear today the voice of the Lord today, who still is the best parent in the world:

Listen: *"The ox knows its owner, and the donkey its master's crib; But Israel does not know, my people do not consider." Alas, sinful nation, a people laden with iniquity, a brood of evildoers, children who are corrupters! They have forsaken the LORD, they have provoked to anger The Holy One of Israel, they have turned away backward."*

Pray: Lord, please forgive us our sin, and the sins of our children and please keep leading us all, in the Way everlasting, in Jesus name we ask it, amen.

Night-Whisper | **BELIEVE**

Lousy Anna or Louisiana?

Isaiah 55:1

"Ho! Everyone who thirsts, Come to the waters; And you who have no money, come, buy and eat. Yes, come, buy wine and milk Without money and without price." NKJV

When God made me, I was born with what my father often referred to as, "Ducks Disease". In other words, my backside was very close to the ground or, to put it another way, I'm not very tall! Subsequently, over the years I have learnt when looking for clothes, that if they fit my distinct proportions of person and pocket, then it's best to buy two of them right that very minute, as in the long run it will save both time and money.

There was once an indiscriminate woman of purchase, who always spent too much for things that were worth far less. Anna was her name and her infamous fiscal failings led to many items which she purchased to be found in the end to be of no real value whatsoever. These seeming worthless purchases and one large one in particular, have lately been referred to as "The Lousy Anna Purchase".

Today in 1803, US envoys agreed to pay $11,250,000 together with assumed claims of its citizens against France, in the amount of $3,750,000, to purchase what was then known as, "The Louisiana Territory". It appears Napoleon Bonaparte needed money for, shall we say, other endeavors more pressing at home. So, young America acquired 828,000 acres of Louisiana Territory for the bargain price of less than three cents an acre. In the end, 13 States would be carved from this vast piece of land. Friends, it would appear that it's good to know when to sell but when it's time to buy, then buy, buy, buy! What a fantastic Louisiana purchase that was!

What do you do though, when a bargain comes around and you don't have the money to buy it? Well, you either sell what you have to raise the necessary capital, or loan the money from some kind of a lender. Either way, speedy purchases can be a bit of a gamble and often times, quick sales are like buying a pig in a poke. Imagine then an offer to purchase and consequently an offer to own, something vast and immeasurably valuable that will in fact only cost you but one thing to buy. Yes, what if the cost of such a fantastic purchase was quite simply, just thirst!

Imagine as well that this treasure you purchase with your thirst, exceeds in beauty, magnitude, return, desirability, expanse, depth, color, height, length, breadth, fragrance, climate, consideration, welcome and wonder! Indeed, exceeds all that you can possibly imagine or think! That would be some kind of bargain

Friends, it would appear that it's good to know when to sell but when it's time to buy, then buy, buy, buy!

wouldn't it? Indeed, you would be a fool not to obtain such a satisfying commodity!

So then friends, tell me today, why are you so quickly spending, your hard earned money on that which does not satisfy, on that which passes away? Get thirsty, then get God and all the promises that go with Him!

Listen: *"Listen carefully to Me, and eat what is good, and let your soul delight itself in abundance. Incline your ear, and come to Me. Hear, and your soul shall live; and I will make an everlasting covenant with you even the sure mercies of David." Isaiah 55:2-3*

Pray: Lord, make me so thirsty that I will have enough to buy all I can from You. Lord give me Your eternal currency and then come satisfy my thirsty soul! Help me make some fantastic Louisiana purchase today, instead of my many lousy Anna ones! Amen and Amen!

PAUSE FOR PRAYER | 66CITIES

Well, I do pray that the first month of this quarter of NightWhispers written with you in mind, have prospered you spiritually and pushed you on a little farther down the road in knowing, obeying and immediately following the commands of the God of the whole Bible. This is my desire.

I am Victor Robert Farrell and I am the author of Night-Whispers. I also have the privilege of being the President of The 66 Books Ministry and I want to tell you a little bit about our major project which is: 66Cities. I believe one of the problems with the rapid moral decline of the West coupled with the influx of other religions, has been the compromise of the local church. It is as though we leaders have watered down the wine of the Gospel with the methods and culture of the world and have done so to such an extent that all we are left with is an anemic and slightly rose colored, fluoride-filled cup of poor tepid mouth wash. It is good for nothing except to be poured down the drain. This compromise I speak of, was to stop speaking about the God of the whole Bible and to such an extent that Christians were left in a strange kind of idolatry, worshiping the God of a cultural constructed Christianity, and so much so, that when these same Christians came into contact with the real God of the Bible, He troubled them and offended them. Indeed, they were embarrassed by Him and wanted Him excluded from their parties. The world of course, found more substance in the other gods, especially that kind of unbiblical Trinitarian spirituality which allowed science and hedonism to mate with the X factor of their own particular choosing.

We at The 66 Books Ministry intend to preach the Gospel of Jesus Christ and the God of the whole Bible, from each of the 66 Books of the Bible in the 66 most influential cities of the nations of the world. That's 16,500 cities in an annual and ongoing basis. To make this happen we are prayerfully raising up teams of proclaimers and 'prayer rangers' to go into these cities. We see this is a true prophetic witness to the glory of God. Indeed. This is the main reason why we are doing this: that God the Father and God the Son may be seen and Glorified in the power of God The Holy Spirit. We hope and pray, that many will see the Father, trust in the Son and be saved by the power of the Holy Spirit as well. Brethren, **we covet your prayers as we do this.** Check out WWW.66Books.TV

Night-Whisper | **WATCH**

Google's gatekeeper

T he mathematical constant "e" was in fact the 2005 corresponding value of the planned share offering of $2,718,281,828 for the popular internet search engine Google. For sure, Google is a quirky company with some quirky founders! Indeed, Larry Page and Sergey Brin said that Google was not a conventional company at all but rather was a company that "does good things for the world even if we forgo some short term gains". This statement is found in a letter explaining Google's company policies under the title of, "do no evil". I like that.

2 Corinthians 13:7

Now I pray to God that you do no evil, not that we should appear approved, but that you should do what is honorable, NKJV

Emotional, business, racial, political, material or territorial war, mostly brings out the worst in human beings. From Muslims murdering contractors and defiling their dead bodies, to Christians from Western armed forces, torturing and abusing its prisoners, it is evident that once again, what is within us human beings, manifests itself in terrible ways once the moral gatekeepers of our societies are removed.

The apostle Paul, himself a lover and proclaimer of God's unmerited favor and forgiveness, so lavishly and lovingly poured upon us open gated sinners through the merits of the substitutionary death of Jesus, to make us now forgiven and fully at one with the Father, well, even he still confessed, that he was a walking battleground! "For the good that I will to do, I do not do; but the evil I will not to do, that I practice... But I see another law in my members, warring against the law of my mind, and bringing me into captivity to the law of sin which is in my members. O wretched man that I am! Who will deliver me from this body of death? I thank God through Jesus Christ our Lord!" (Romans 7:19-25). Paul says that Jesus is the ultimate and only answer to this overwhelming internal war. However friends, until Jesus enters into the hearts of men, the Father has provided society with certain gatekeepers, to keep sin somewhat restrained. We need to thank God that we have seen a gatekeeper in Google and pray that God will set many more watchmen on the walls, of the many and much plundered and starving societies in which we live.

Google set a watchman upon its wall called "do no evil." Tell me, how might you become a similar gatekeeper in your society today?

Listen: *"He has shown you, O man, what is good; And what does the LORD require of you But to do justly, To love mercy, And to walk humbly with your God?" Micah 6:8*

Pray: Lord, help us set up the watchmen of our society once more and let them shout! Lord, lock the gates, until monstrous sin is stilled and killed, and poor heart is replaced by great heart victorious, The Lord Jesus Christ Himself. Amen!

Night-Whisper | **CHOOSE**

Clinging to corpses

I t's North Americans only marsupial and famous for playing dead. The small unglamorous creature with big black eyes, a pale pointy face and a hairless rat like tail, can become so stressed, that it goes into shock and quite simply, passes out! Such action may stop predators chasing it but unfortunately, the already seemingly limp and lifeless body takes away from some car drivers the need to swerve.

Revelation 3:18c

...and anoint your eyes with eye salve, that you may see. NKJV

This Opossum I found wasn't playing dead now. It lay at the side of the road, stiff and sodden with rain. Perched atop the poor corpse were two five-inch babies, shivering and wretched, trying to get what warmth was left from their poor dead mother. A visit to the vet, a warm box, and a surgical glove filled with hot water to act as a warm body, a little cat food and in just a few hours, the orphaned baby Opossums were bright eyed and running about. They are the most freakiest looking little things. Imagine a smelly 'Clanger' drunk and with teeth. That's what a baby Opossum looks like.

In a similar vein, I heard on the news quite recently of an "odious smell coming from a vehicle" which had been left in the car park of a large food store. Investigation found the dead body of someone else's mother, still buckled into the passenger seat. Her daughter had been driving around with her for five days like that and had just popped in to get some provisions, leaving her mom waiting in the car! It was gruesomely obvious that the poor daughter was both sad and sick.

I remember speaking to some church planters in a large American inner city. Some of that denominations dying congregations in the area have both facilities and finances that make outreach to the emerging generation a real and exciting possibility. In addition to that, many local large and successful suburban churches have personnel and resources ready to come alongside and help with a fresh attack against the gates of hell in the inner cities. Unfortunately, the tiny and shivering congregations sheltering themselves in the memories of their great and once glorious past, are either like the baby marsupials I found on the side of the road, frightened and too desperate to move, or like the sad daughter driving her mother's copse around, very sick indeed. They are still adamant in their loss and madness and so still clinging to the lifeless corpse of a church that was once, long ago, thriving.

Like the daughter driving around her dead mother, many of our churches are refusing to accept the facts of their demise and are still willing to live with the increasing smell of death..

Like the daughter driving around her dead mother, many of our churches are refusing to accept the facts of their demise and are still willing to live with the increasing smell of death. Soon, some group or philanthropist shall turn their remains into a neatly prepared Cadaver.

Friends, it's time to get off the corpse and bury the dead.

Listen: *"I call heaven and earth as witnesses today against you, that I have set before you life and death, blessing and cursing; therefore choose life, that both you and your descendants may live;" Deuteronomy 30:19*

Pray: Be it ever so hard, help me this day O Lord, to choose life!

| Vol 02 | Q2 | NW00490| May 03rd |

Night-Whisper | **SATISFY**

Simple yet sumptuous

Everyone knows that when Henry Ford first mass-produced his Model T Ford, you could have it any color you wanted provided it was black! Today of course, Mr. "Monotone" Ford would not have been able to compete in this vast market place of color choice.

Matthew 11:29

"Take My yoke upon you and learn from Me, for I am gentle and lowly in heart, and you will find rest for your souls. For My yoke is easy and My burden is light." NKJV

Whenever I go down to the local supermarket it is not long before I become overwhelmed with the array of choice that is set before me. For me to be found perplexed in the aisle of most any shop nowadays is not unusual, as on average, each store has some 50,000 separate items to choose from! From the vast array of competing service providers and all their sumptuous socks in sizzling and saucy colors that the marketing mantra of the century is indeed, "competition afforded by choice".

Churches both large and small have spotted this seeming need to provide choice to seekers of spiritual truth and have unwittingly engaged themselves in that self-same competition afforded by the lust for choice! So, on most weekends you will find churches offering services on Saturday and Sunday, Monday morning, various afternoons and most evenings, contemporary and traditional, long and short, dressed up, dressed down, smells bells and hope on a rope. I'm not knocking it; after all it is getting in the punters! After all, people expect choice and are coming to worship and to participate in the style of their choice on the day of their choice at the time of their choice. Indeed, it's so needful now in Christendom to present such spiritual choice, such spiritual options that today, this service choice has been represented to us as the Christian norm, even the cutting edge of postmodern evangelism! After all, look at all the choice in the availability of the multitude of protestant

denominations, and hey, didn't Paul say that he would become all things to all men if by any means he could win some, and by the way haven't we got four different Gospels with one message, you know four different flavors with a different emphasis for at least four different sets of audiences? Good grief isn't it obvious,
God is into choice!

Laying aside the honorable and dutiful question of which day of the week to gather as a body to adore God together and to minister to one another; laying aside the exceptionally cheap mile wide and inch deep quality of such a present

The real sheep are left rotting on the hills and wasting away for lack of good nutrition.

day presentation of spiritual choice; laying aside the market place competition set by postmodern day consumer Christianity; laying aside the subsequent "Wal-Marting" of Christendom, we still come to another massive problem for the sheep of His pasture and that is, that although the postmodern spiritual punter may easily quench his natural curiosity, may easily sign up for his shopping reward card and get the nice little spiritual discount his truly unrepentant soul requires, the real sheep are left rotting on the hills and wasting away for lack of good nutrition. Such choosing, such foul presentation of choice, such pandering to the flesh, for that is what it is, has left in its wake an emaciated Christianity that now teeters and totters pathetically through the land. The spiritual punters have touched and tasted and are some are even satisfied with the tasteless drivel, as after all, it would appear that being a Christian is not as demanding as they thought it might be. However, the people of His pasture, are left both hungry and starving.

Sheep you see, don't want choice; they just want feeding the food that is fitted for their needs! True sheep just want to eat! Crispy or grilled, they just don't care! They don't want fries, and they don't want coke with it and no, they apparently don't want honey mustard either! Good grief they just want a burger in a bun! They just want food from a shepherd who is sprinkled with the anointing from on high and glows with the manifest presence of the Savior. I tell you what: sheep will travel a thousand miles for such simple and sumptuous fare and you know what, they may even do it on a Sunday mate. Imagine that!

Listen: *"Stand in the ways and see, and ask for the old paths, where the good way is, and walk in it; then you will find rest for your souls." Jeremiah 6:16*

Pray: Grant me O good Shepherd, a simplicity of life, a focus on the fundamentals and then O my God, come quench my thirsty soul and feed me with the food allotted to me. Amen!

| Vol 02 | Q2 | NW00491 | May 04th |

Night-Whisper | **MERCY**

Makers mark

Margaret Hilda Roberts an Oxford graduate, became the first woman to be president of one of the University's political organizations. After marrying Dennis and giving birth to twins, she restarted her political career and ended up being elected for three terms as the first woman Prime Minister of the United Kingdom and Northern Ireland and today in 1974, she was sworn in after her first election victory.

1 Kings 12:19

So Israel has been in rebellion against the house of David to this day. NKJV

Rightly or wrongly, Hilda began dismantling socialism in Britain. Her unwavering resolution to stand by her political decisions and policies in face of war, trade union conflict and terrorist bombing led her to be dubbed the "Iron Lady". However, the hurt, sense of loss, and grievance that many people in the country felt during her terms of office by the implementation of her policies, which meant they lost their health care, money in their pockets, their jobs and communities, have led her memory to be regarded with not a little infamy in her homeland. "Thatcherism," that form of politics attributed to her style and philosophy, is now only repeated with spitting disdain. Never the less, because of the vast electoral majority Mrs. Thatcher received in her parliaments, she was allowed very wide parameters of operation and implementation. Subsequently then, no matter what you think of her, Britain was never the same after Hilda held the high ground.

Here is a lesson friends. A majority does not make you right. A majority does not make you righteous. A majority does not make you wise. A majority does not make you gracious. A majority does not mean peace, neither is it necessarily harmonious. Remember folks that democracy means majority rule and not necessarily righteous and therefore merciful rule! Kings, queens, presidents, prime ministers, bishops, elders, CEOs, committees, husbands, parents, big brothers, senior pastors and leaders all and of every kind, always need to remember mercy.

Mercy, that kindly ministry of love, that real spiritual brew, that true "Makers Mark" if you will, that revival drink that makes cold hearts warm, hard ground soft and hate to dissipate, oh yes, that most magnificent mercy, should be the Master's mark on the forehead of every Christian leader. True ministers of God then, either church or secular, are direct ministers of the Almighty Father and need to remember that He is called, the "Father of Mercies". Make sure your hands, eyes, heart and mouth all bear the Maker's Mark today.

Listen: *"Blessed are the merciful, for they shall obtain mercy." Matthew 5:7*

Pray: Lord, temper my personal power with both marvelous and melting mercy, in Jesus name I pray, Amen!

Night-Whisper | **HONOR**

Coaching Columbus

So she says, "Hey! We should have taken a left back there!" He doesn't reply but inside he's thinking, "Christopher Columbus didn't need directions and neither do I!" Such are the thoughts of everyman in the driving seat when any woman, wife or otherwise, attempts to give him some dimensional direction. Call it chauvinism, call it childishness, call it instability, call it even God's design; yes, call it lack of security, or call it what you want but accept this fact and make peace with it, "Men are just like that!" I mean, what can women tell them about finding directions?

1 Peter 3:5,6

For in this manner, in former times, the holy women who trusted in God also adorned themselves, being submissive to their own husbands, as Sarah obeyed Abraham, calling him Lord.NKJV

Unfortunately, this male attitude does not translate well when the opposite sex also tries to give any non-dimensional direction to them. Men will rarely sit peaceably under the authority and teaching of a woman. On the odd occasion, they might listen to and follow a Royal Queen, a Boudicca, a Deborah, an Elizabeth or maybe even a Margaret! However, it's rare friends, it's so very rare. Women have to be seen to have wisdom, age, respect, maybe even a kind of motherhood but preferably a grandparenthood about them, before men will even countenance some good advice from their lips. You will forgive my lack of political correctness here I hope, because my New Year's resolution was to stop putting square pegs into round holes and just face some plain old facts, even if they are contrary to popular politically correct opinion! My statements reflect nothing on the abilities of women but on everything to do with being a man. Yes, don't get me wrong, for every wise husband learns that he should listen to his wife. After all, she's usually correct!

May I suggest the failure of women to communicate and instruct men is not so much in the content of what is said but in the delivery. Not so much in the rightness but in the approach. The male ego is a fragile commodity remember, and needs treating with honor and respect. If you don't, then women, you will not be received. End of story.

The benefits of honorable communication from women to men are however, far reaching, even reaching into the future. Ask any mother and they will tell you that there comes a point when their loving son will not listen to a word they say! Nevertheless, ask any man, and they shall tell you that when sensibility eventually came upon them, they remembered and cherished every word spoken from the loving lips of mothers and grandmothers. Yes, every passionate plea and every overheard heard prayer became to them a means of re-instruction, a treasure of remembered love that repeated itself in their more mature days. Such honorable instruction as this, will be respectfully received, recovered, and regurgitated. Men are just like that and you dear sisters would do well to take note.

May I suggest the failure of women to communicate and instruct men is not so much in the content of what is said but in the delivery..

Listen: *"When I call to remembrance the genuine faith that is in you, which dwelt first in your grandmother Lois and your mother Eunice, and I am persuaded is in you also." 2 Tim 1:4-5*

Pray: Thank you Lord Jesus, for the great and honorable and courageous women in the Kingdom of God. What would we do without them Lord? Make them wise toward men. Now O Lord, help the men of the Kingdom glory in their manhood, in Jesus amen we pray, amen.

Night-Whisper | **PERSEVERE**

Finger Fighting

One night, I channel hopped between two performances of "Alison Crouch and Union Station" and the "Russian Ballet" and well, with all that singing and dancing, a lovely sunset evening, a hot cup of tea and a box of chocolate caramels in my hand, I thought I had finally arrived!

Daniel 1:5

And the king appointed for them a daily provision of the king's delicacies and of the wine which he drank, and three years of training for them, so that at the end of that time they might serve before the king. NKJV

Having had years of practice, I have found that I have become pretty adept at combining eating and drinking, I mean I can do it with no problems at all. It's smooth, it's tasty and only on occasion do I spill stuff down my shirt! Ah, but when it comes to successfully combining music and dance in a most satisfying way, well, I am not so good at it. In fact, I'm rubbish.

As I observed the Bolshoi Ballet, it was obvious that I needed more instruction on the old song and dance front, so I popped in another caramel hopped over to the other channel and listened longingly at the wonderful sounds so effortlessly produced by the awesome band of Union Station, flicked back again to the other channel and stared at the magnificent movements, so muscularly controlled and expertly executed by the Bolshoi. All this singing and dancing was made to look so simple, so effortless! Unfortunately, we know friends that for every minute of winsome wonder, whether from vocal chords or limbered thighs, there lies, years and years of tough old training. And there we have it. Training!

The need for tough old training in spiritual matters is equally important for you cannot "desire or will" yourself into Godliness, you cannot "faith" yourself into sin overcoming victory, no, you need to be trained to overcome it. Even the young lion, bear, and giant killer David, blessed the Lord his Rock who "trained *his hands for war and his fingers for battle." (Psalm 144:1).* Yes, God focused His training on even and especially David's little fingers and in the so doing, made them mighty!

I wonder if you have ever considered that one of God the Holy Spirit's jobs with you is that of being a personal trainer, a life coach if you will, where He is orchestrating events and providentially providing you with challenges to purposely pump up those legs of righteousness and faith, make big those arms of mercy and expand those biceps of love, strengthen the hold of those hands of kindness and patience and build an eternal grip in those fingers of gentleness and long-suffering. Yes sir, love, mercy, faith, gentleness and longsuffering may all be fruits of the Holy Spirit, but all of His fruits and all of His gifts only ripen and grow over time, and then only through much tough training.

All of the Holy Spirit's fruits and all of His gifts only ripen and grow over time, and then only through much tough training.

So get of that couch of defeat today you poor and pitiful potato and once and for all, lay aside those caramels of carnal apathy! Up and at 'em people, for you have far from arrived! Be sure to make the most of your God ordained tough old spiritual training today. Yes! It's God who is at work in you.

Listen: *"And He spoke a parable to them: 'Can the blind lead the blind? Will they not both fall into the ditch? A disciple is not above his teacher, but everyone who is perfectly trained will be like his teacher.'" Luke 6:39-40*

Pray: - Lord, make me fit and able, ready for every good work. In Jesus name I ask it, amen.

Night-Whisper | **FAITHFULNESS**

Faithful failures?

Reputed by many to be one of the best theological thinkers of his time; referred to as the "Bloom of Puritanism" by Dr ML Jones; hero of the faith, ignition point for the great awakening, missionary to Housatonic Indians and president of Princeton University, Jonathan Edwards was never the less voted out of his church after 23 years of service, and 1,200 sermons! The vote was 200 to 23 against him. Astonishing.

1 Corinthians 4:4,5

But He who judges me is the Lord. Therefore judge nothing before the time. KJV

On a similar note, I am always encouraged when I read about those Old Testament scallywags, which we sometimes pompously refer to as "heroes of the faith!" For you see today, we would throw most of them out of our churches and that's the truth. So, you can see how it makes me giggle when I hear them so lovingly referenced! Honestly, I truly believe if God hadn't mentioned many of them in Hebrews 11, as being heroes in His eyes, then by today's standards of measuring acceptable Christian giants, we would have written off the vast majority of them as fantastic failures, each one of them possessing tremendous individual shortcomings and seemingly gigantic impediments that no respectable Christian should ever possess in today's church. Undoubtedly, at some point these heroes of faith, like Jonathan Edwards, would be voted out of their churches and regarded as failed as leaders.

However, understanding seeming failure is really not so simple. I wonder if at the great assizes what we see now as failure may indeed be judged otherwise? Paul seemed to think so when he says, *"It is a very small thing that I should be judged by you or by a human court" (1 Cor 4:3).* You see, *leadership* is in fact a triple mix of leader, followers and circumstance and failure in any of these variables, can make or break the person up front, the person at the point, the sharp end, occupying the main leadership position. In this triple mix, some circumstances and some followers may be outside of your control you see. Edwards found that out and I tell you, Edwards was no failure!

Friends I speak to us all today then, for we all lead in some capacity, when I tell you that I am increasingly convinced of three things:

Leadership is in fact a triple mix of leader, followers and circumstance and failure in any of these variables, can make or break the person up front.

First, that we all are imperfect human beings. So lighten up on leaders.

Second, repentance, growth and change are continual processes for us all, especially leaders. With your prayers and your encouragement, with your grace and with your favor, and especially with your support, your leaders will improve!

Thirdly and most importantly, that we followers can help leaders lead, can make leaders great, can invest and ensure the success of leadership. Yes, followers can make or break leaders. Think about that.

Listen: *"Obey your leaders and follow their orders. They watch over your souls without resting, since they must give to God an account of their service. If you obey them, they will do their work gladly; if not, they will do it with sadness, and that would be of no help to you." Hebrews 13:17 TEV*

Pray: Lord help us followers to make great our loving leaders, in Jesus name I pray, amen!

Night-Whisper | **PRIORITIES**

Ichabod

1 Samuel 2:30

For those who honor Me I will honor, and those who despise Me shall be lightly esteemed. NKJV

Who could forget the scene in that great film *Chariots of Fire* where the main character, Eric Liddell, preparing to run in the Olympic final which by the way, was a race he had not trained for, just before he gets on his mark, is handed a piece of paper with the Bible text above written upon it. Marvelous! You see, having forfeited the opportunity to race the 100 meters because it was on a Sunday, Liddell faced down an earthly king, and the howling press all baying for his blood, indeed, he shouldered pressure from all quarters to compete in the 100 meters final which was to be held on a Sunday, and despite the weight upon him he did not cave in but instead said no, and put God first. Now, according to the note, God would honor him for his stand. Of course, like all great stories in history, Liddell went on to win the 400-metre final!

Eric Liddell was undoubtedly an honored and true champion in every sense of the word but whether he was given the piece of paper with that particular Bible text, is highly unlikely. Nevertheless, the truth and fulfillment of those words stands as certain and as immovable as the Mount of the Most High God.

However, I do need to tell you friends that the Biblical context of this verse is couched in horror rather than in glory. You see, Eli, the then High priest, Eli, had not put God first with respect to his two sons Hophni and Phinehas. No, this dirty duo had consistently coerced from the congregation the best and largest portions of food and by religious bullying, had made themselves rich, licentious and odious. Eli, in turn had compounded their sin in allowing them to continue to abuse their office and the people they were serving and in so doing, had caused Israel to hate the worship and offering commanded by God. Eli had honored his sons before God and God was not well pleased. In return for this "lightly esteeming" of the Lord, God then "lightly esteemed" Eli and cut short His original promise of honor and blessing to Eli's family line. God was going to kill his sons you see, and in the future, all of his male descendants would die in the prime of their life; their offspring, consuming their parent's eyes and grieving their hearts; whilst they languished in poverty, begging to serve as priests just for the smallest portions of food. Truly, God's glorious blessing had departed from the family line of Eli. Why? *"...for those who honor Me I will honor, and those who despise Me shall be lightly esteemed."*

The Biblical context of this verse is couched in horror rather than in glory..

Tell me, how are you maybe lightly esteeming the Lord?

Listen: *"Therefore we must give the more earnest heed to the things we have heard, lest we drift away. For if the word spoken through angels proved steadfast, and every transgression and disobedience received a just reward, how shall we escape if we neglect so great a salvation, which at the first began to be spoken by the Lord, and was confirmed to us by those who heard Him, God also bearing witness both with signs and wonders, with various miracles, and gifts of the Holy Spirit, according to His own will?" Hebrews 2:1-4*

Pray: Living God, help me to put You and Your kingdom and You and Your honor, first in my life. Indeed, help me to put You and Your glory even before the very desire of my eyes. Amen.

| Vol 02 | Q2 | NW00496 | May 09th |

Night-Whisper | **TRUST**

Money and money's worth

As all royalty would be approached in the East, these Kings, these most marvelous Magi, opened up their treasure boxes and presented to the greatest King, God over all, the most valuable of their countries then commercial products. No doubt, these gifts were emblematic; no doubt, these gifts were prophetic as well in that they spoke of the purpose and destiny of the tiny little lamb then so sweetly set before them. However, my question today is this: "What happened to the gifts?"

Matthew 2:11

And when they had opened their treasures, they presented gifts to Him: gold, frankincense, and myrrh. NKJV

You would agree with me I am sure, that you don't travel over vast distances with the hope of finding someone you have searched and longed to see, without taking with you something of exceptional worth and value. So, I assume then that this was pretty expensive stuff! Yet I am not aware of any archaeological searches for the "lost gold of Jesus" or the "perfume of the Prince of life". No, this treasure is never spoken of again. Why? Well that old and great commentator Matthew Henry, gives us a very simple statement that the gifts were essentially "money and money's worth" and that's very helpful. You see in effect, Mary and Joseph were given a universal commodity of exchange. It was the Euro or the Dollar of the day if you will and they were going to need it!

The verses following in Matthew shows the fearful family, fleeing from Herod and hiding in Egypt until his death, before then returning to Israel, the long way home. Arriving back in Nazareth, they would start afresh in beginning to support themselves. All of this coming and going, stopping and starting, ending and beginning, breaking and building, took money. It was an expensive exercise!

We can take great encouragement in that the long and expensive journey of Jesus, Joseph and Mary were taken care of by the Father in advance of it happening. My goodness! The Father even brought precious provision and finances from afar, to ensure the protection and establishment of the family. So, where are the gifts? Well, I would suggest friends, that they were all, very quickly and very well spent! God gives us treasure for spending, even for the financing of all our journeying. It is never for hoarding. Remember that.

God gives us treasure for spending, even for the financing of all our journeying. It is never for hoarding..

Listen: *"Therefore do not worry, saying, 'What shall we eat?' or 'What shall we drink?' or 'What shall we wear?' For after all these things the Gentiles seek. For your heavenly Father knows that you need all these things. But seek first the kingdom of God and His righteousness, and all these things shall be added to you. Therefore do not worry about tomorrow, for tomorrow will worry about its own things. Sufficient for the day is its own trouble." Matt 6:31-34*

Pray: Living God, help me to put You and Your kingdom first and then see You come up with all my various expenses. Amen!

Naked love

S ir Edward Dyer, Elizabethan poet, in his poem "Love is Love" finishes the first of just two stanzas with these words: -

Seas have their source, and so have shallow springs;
And love is love, in beggars and in kings.

Luke 21:2-4

He saw also a certain poor widow putting in two mites. So He said, "Truly I say to you that this poor widow has put in more than all; for all these out of their abundance have put in offerings for God, but she out of her poverty put in all the livelihood that she had."NKJV

How sweet. However, do tell me friends: who would you rather be loved by? A beggar or a King? It's an important question for Dyer says there is no difference in the quality and quantity of love from either personage. Surely, this is a truth of biblical proportion and comfort? However, there are a number of problems with this acceptance of no differentiation between the love of a beggar and the love of a king.

Consider first, two families living in the same street and both have a dearly loved child. Over the years, the father of one family has the skill and opportunity to excel in the workplace and increase his financial base substantially. The other has skill and commitment but lacking opportunity due to the mismanagement of others, means that he has struggled just to keep a roof over their heads! When the children of these two families reach leaving age, one loving parent gives a car and a college fund to his children, the other one gives an apology. "Seas have their source, and so have shallow springs; and love is love, in beggars and in kings." Maybe, but in this case, who would the child have better been loved by? A beggar or a king?

Or how about this: imagine two married couples, both deeply in love. One couple holidays annually, eats out regularly and buys one another thoughtful and expensive gifts. The other couple occasionally orders

Pizza, rarely goes anywhere and make their own cards to send to one another on their birthdays. They get by. However, tell me friends, would you rather be loved by a beggar or a king? Does it matter?

You cannot buy love, neither can you sell love, for love does not need a Porsche to carry itself to someone's heart.

Though I do believe Dyer to be correct, nevertheless, a king can afford a whole together more material and practical expression of that same quality and quantity of love found in beggars. In this material world, such king like material expression of love, can also be seen and felt and yes, it does make life that much easier and living that much nicer. That's just a fact.

Nevertheless, money's not everything, though it can get you most things and it can buy you a good amount of happiness and provide you with a substantial amount of freedom. Yes indeed, money is a great key to freedom of every kind but money is not everything and thank God for that, for most people are not kings in their own financial world.

It seems to me then, that if indeed, Dyer is correct, then love has to run deeper, farther and longer than anything money can buy. I mean anything! For true love possesses an eternal quality and in its truest form has to be communicated in faith. Have you got that? True love has to be communicated in faith. In this respect maybe, beggars have the opportunity to express a purer and truer love, more than kings could ever do. For true love driven by faith, prayerfully and continually commits the beloved to God the good and God the great, while watching for and prayerfully pushing for both the spiritual and material goodness, grace and mercy of God, to be mightily manifest in the lives of those they truly love. Yes, I wonder if beggars have the opportunity to love deeper and purer whilst by faith, always beaming sunlight shafts of prayer into the lives of those they wish to bless but at the moment, cannot bless themselves. Do you see that possibility?

Naked love, disrobed of wealth, has to find eternal conduits of expression rather than the easy and earthly material ones that money can so easily buy. I tell you now friends, you cannot buy love, neither can you sell love, for love does not need a Porsche to carry itself to someone's heart. Think about that, for yes indeed, "Seas have their source, and so have shallow springs; And love is love, in beggars and in kings."

Listen: *"For you know the grace of our Lord Jesus Christ, that though He was rich, yet for your sakes He became poor, that you through His poverty might become rich." 2 Cor 8:9*

Pray: Loving God, give my love, both   eternal roots and eternal consequences, in Jesus name I ask it, amen!

Night-Whisper | **LISTEN**

I'm 1812, with a bullet

By comparison America has had four incidents and Britain only one. This morning in 1812 in England, Spencer Percival told his wife that he had dreamt the previous night that he was shot whilst in the House of Commons by a man wearing a green coat with brass buttons. His family tried to dissuade Percival, the then Prime Minister, from going to the House but the call of duty and the need to answer pressing questions of policy, both at home and abroad, called the Prime Minister to work.

Matthew 2:12

Then, being divinely warned in a dream that they should not return to Herod, they departed for their own country another way. NKJV

John Bellingham, who had claimed he had not received remuneration for work he had done in Russia on behalf of the crown and quietly insane with the losses that he claimed had been brought upon him by the government, calmly shot the Prime Minster through the heart and killed him. Bellingham was tried and just seven days later, was hung in front of Newgate prison.

Had Spencer Percival took note of the dream, no doubt he may have lived a lot longer and history may have been substantially changed. However, he ignored the premonition, the warning, the message, and consequently was killed.

Was this a message from God to someone who is reported to have been an "evangelical Prime Minister"? Should he have listened? After all, what would you have done? If he had shared this dream with anyone other than his family and refused to have gone to work that day, no doubt he would have been classed as losing his marbles as well! Really, what can we make of these things? Maybe, we can at least modify Shakespeare and say, "There are more things in heaven and earth, Horatio, that are dreamt of." Think about it. Some dreams are worth listening to.

Listen: *"Now when they had departed, behold, an angel of the Lord appeared to Joseph in a dream, saying, 'Arise, take the young child and His mother, flee to Egypt, and stay there until I bring you word; for Herod will seek the young Child to destroy Him.'" Matthew 2:13*

Pray: Lord, make me attentive to Your communications to me. Amen!

Night-Whisper | **BE**

Rattling back together

Most certainly, Jesus eulogizes John the Baptist in a most loving and wonderful way. "John," He says, "is more than a prophet!" The honor, specialness, uniqueness, importance, of the messenger of God, the Way preparer, is beyond question. Yet, he who is least in the Kingdom of God is greater than he! What does that mean?

Luke 7:24-27

.. "What did you go out into the wilderness to see? A reed shaken by the wind? But what did you go out to see? A man clothed in soft garments? Indeed those who are gorgeously appareled and live in luxury are in kings' courts. But what did you go out to see? A prophet? Yes, I say to you, and more than a prophet. This is he of whom it is written: 'Behold, I send My messenger before Your face, Who will prepare Your way before You.' For I say to you, among those born of women there is not a greater prophet than John the Baptist; but he who is least in the kingdom of God is greater than he." NKJV

Note first that there are gradations in the Kingdom of God. There is the least and there is the greatest. At the top we know there shall be near co-regents who shall sit at the left and right of Christ and we also know of the 24 elders around the throne, and as the angels differ in rank and category and substance, I have no doubt that the elect shall do the same. I believe the bride of Christ shall have its least and its greatest, shall have its members acknowledged in substance rank and category. The apportioning of reward, and the dominion of crowning at the judgement seat of Christ shall no doubt reflect this. Suffice to say, there shall be greatest and there shall be least in the Kingdom of God.

It has been said that the answer to the world's problems in the past has always come from the womb of a woman. The abattoirs of murderous abortion, destroy many of God's answers to the worlds prayers. John was the greatest prophet of anyone born of women. He is the tops!

Now then, you could say that Jesus, the begotten of the father, the great servant King of all the redeemed, is least and therefore greatest in the Kingdom of God. As the least, Jesus then is greater than the greatest human prophet, John the Baptist. Well, I can war that, but Oh my goodness, it took some hermeneutical gymnastics to get there! However, I think that there is a clearer and a better understanding though.

Those born of the Holy Spirit of God become 'Divinely human.'

Look now, those members of the church, the body of Christ, and this the great Kingdom of God, are born not from below but from above. They are born again by the Holy Spirit of God. These people are the Bride of Christ and they are a new breed, a new class, a new race, a new genre, a new spiritually bio-divers group of the most excellent of God's creation! The 'least of these' born from above, are greater than the greatest of those born of women, even John the Baptist. The question is, both how and in what way are they greater?

Someone has said that those born of the Holy Spirit of God become 'Divinely human.' Only our physical death can separate, we, the Divinely human people from the presence of our remaining sin nature, and once this is done, in the resurrection, in the adoption, we receive a resurrected, reformed, renewed, remade, and all 'revved' up body to better accommodate the Divine humanity which God has made us to be, and these resurrected bodies are shaped to fit the positions of power won by our present faith and fidelity, and those future ruling authorities accorded to us by the Sovereign grace of God. Even so, here below, we who are now made victorious over our sin nature by the blood of Christ, still fight against it whilst in this 'unadopted' body of ours. Never the less, by God's indwelling Holy Spirit, we are still made to be Divinely human, even the sons of God, and being sons, we are part of the Kingdom of God which is within us. In this, we are much greater than John the Baptist.

Surely you would agree then, that such people born from above and greater than John the Baptizer, should have a profound impact on the world? I ask myself this question tonight then, "As someone made Divinely human by the Holy Spirit of God, as someone who is least in the Kingdom of God, in what way am I impacting and changing the world?" As for me, currently, the honest answer seems to be, "very little."

Let us not forget who we are and what we are, for this 'forgetting' is part of the problem. John had a solitary dessert and little distraction to remember who he was. Look now, we have an abundance of distraction and noise to help us forget who we are.

Let us therefore find some desert places in our lives. Let us find some high mountains, let us find some solitary place, let us fond some quiet times out of each 24 hour day to go and pray and in praying to begin to remember who and what we are. I tell you tonight, some of you have forgotten yourself and need a desert to help you remember.

Listen: *There was a man sent from God, whose name was John. This man came for a witness, to bear witness of the Light, that all through him might believe. He was not that Light, but was sent to bear witness of that Light. That was the true Light which gives light to every man coming into the world. He was in the world, and the world was made through Him, and the world did not know Him. He came to His own, and His own did not receive Him. But as many as received Him, to them He gave the right to become children of God, to those who believe in His name: who were born, not of blood, nor of the will of the flesh, nor of the will of man, but of God. (John 1:6-13 NKJV)*

Pray: Father, most days I feel barely human rather than Divinely human. The Cares of this world and the deceitfulness of riches have sucked my spiritual marrow dry. I am a dry bones. Lord, only dry bones can live when Your Holy Spirit rattles me back together. Lord, rattle me back together. Help me find a mountain in a desert, a place by the sea, a vale in the wilderness, that Your breath would re-assemble me and that being so reformed by You, I would remember myself in You. In Jesus name I ask it, amen and let it be so.

Night-Whisper | **FOCUS**

Cross roads and crucial conduits

L eith Anderson in his book, *Leadership That Works*, (page 75) compares the priorities of people of the 1950s with people of today. It's an interesting list:

Yesterday's Priorities	Today's Priorities
Institutional	Individual
Church	Family
Duty	Opportunity
Showing Up	Significance
Faithfulness	Effectiveness

Matthew 4:13 & 17

And leaving Nazareth, He came and dwelt in Capernaum, which is by the sea, in the regions of Zebulun and Naphtali... [f]rom that time Jesus began to preach and to say, "Repent, for the kingdom of heaven is at hand."NKJV

I suppose the danger of such a listing is to assume that people in the 1950s and from that generation, had no real priority for themselves, their families and consequently, had little real personal opportunity, significance or effectiveness? We certainly cannot assume this was the case for Jesus! In planting seeds, He especially took the opportunity to plant effectively, with great present significance and with an even greater future significance.

The Scriptures are clear that Jesus went to Capernaum to fulfill prophecy! A good question then, is why such a town is the subject of such specific prophetic disclosure and Messianic decision? Well, Moody Bible Atlas calls Capernaum, a "Crucial Conduit," and so it was, for "Unlike the sleepy, obscure village of Nazareth, Capernaum was at a crucial Junction, through which coursed a steady stream of humanity from many diverse sectors and countries…it pulsated with the activities and congestion of internationalism."

Interestingly enough folks, though the early apostolic movement surged to the North West, the earliest archaeological evidence of churches are however, found in the North East. Maybe this was due to Jesus taking the opportunity of placing Himself in that crucial conduit of Capernaum which had both great significance and eternal effect?

We all need wisdom in finding and placing ourselves in or at, significant and effective crossroads and crucial conduits!

We all need wisdom in finding and placing ourselves in or at, significant and effective crossroads and crucial conduits! To influence our families, our friends and our world, we must prayerfully seek out these points of cruciality in our physical and spiritual geography, so that we can effectively spread the seed, shine the light, and shake the salt with both eternal significance and infinite effectiveness. Look around and ask yourself, "Is where I am placed today, a crossroads or a conduit? Is where I am standing today, of any real significance and eternal effect? "

Listen: *"Behold, I send you out as sheep in the midst of wolves. Therefore be wise as serpents" Matthew 10:16*

Pray: Lord, help me to box clever and find and position myself in the best place to be for me, my family and the people of the world that You require me to touch. Make me both significant in You and effective in Your mission for me. Amen!

Night-Whisper | **FIGH**T

Beating the big bad burglar

It's an old chorus but I love it. "I went into the enemy's camp and I took back what he stole from me; took back what he stole from me, took back what he stole from me." The truth is friends that we have been robbed and Goliath of Gath, that ugly taunter of the people of God, that giant of a mercenary who mocked Israel on a daily basis and laughed from the haughty hillside at the beautiful people of God, still giggles with glee over our stolen dignity, our stolen strength, our stolen faith, our stolen joy and the consequent and ensuing total inability to fight and be who we are in Jesus, which is, more than conquerors! Today, the big bad burglar still swings his swag bag over his shoulder and shoves our losses down our throat, again and again, scowling at our inability to reclaim what once was ours and our families to enjoy. I'm sick of it! How about you?

Genesis 14:16

So he brought back all the goods, and also brought back his brother Lot and his goods, as well as the women and the people.
NKJV

It was David the youth of faith, who with a stone and sling, toppled that same Goliath and removed his mocking head. It was later at Ziklag when the Amalekites, a continuing symbol for evil and hatred against God's people, came and stole everything of David's and his warriors. Women, children, goods cattle, everything was gone and the remainder was burned with fire! The Scripture reports that the followers of David lifted up their voice and wept until they could weep no more. In addition to that, some of them wanted to stone David, blaming him for everything that had come upon them.

I have been a pastor long enough to know that we can be just like David's robbed warriors. Yes, we are all capable of the same thoughts, feelings and actions towards God, after we too have lit the same burning pyres of grief, despair, despondency and anger in our own hearts. I would suggest that we have even had that same murderous heart towards the greater David, when we have found ourselves staring over the smoldering ruins of dreams and desires that have been stolen from us. It's scary, but true. We can be just like that.

Friends, enough of blaming God! Enough of such debilitation. Enough!

Friends, enough of blaming God! Enough of such debilitation. Enough!

Do you know that the greater David wants you, along with Him, to pursue the big bad burglar and recover, reclaim, restore, and redeem, along with Him, all that has been stolen from you? Everything! Do you believe that? Well you must believe that, and you must believe it today! Be a Rottweiler, lay hold and sink your teeth into that great truth! Be a terrier, don't let go and take back, rip back, what he's stolen from you! Oh and while you're there, give the burglars backside a good ole chompin from me will you! Go get him tiger!

Listen: *"Pursue, for you shall surely overtake them and without fail recover all." 1 Samuel 30:8*

"And nothing of theirs was lacking, either small or great, sons or daughters, spoil or anything which they had taken from them; David recovered all." 1 Samuel 30:19

Pray: Lord, I believe. Help my unbelief. Today with You, I shall rise up and begin the recovery fight, the recovery process, of all that has been stolen from me and from mine. With your help dear Jesus, this shall indeed be done. Amen!

| Vol 02 | Q2 | NW00502 | May 15ᵗʰ |

Night-Whisper | **PERSEVERANCE**

Fighting the flow

P eer pressure is a most powerful force. When a community has an ethos, a world view, an approach, a belief that is widely accepted espoused and adhered to by the vast majority within it and you choose to go against it, disagree with it and even confront it; then friends, you can guarantee that a problem will arise and of course that problem will be you!

John 10:20

And many of them said, "He has a demon and is mad. Why do you listen to Him?"NKJV

Jesus, even in His miracles and teachings had Psalm 69:8 fulfilled amongst His nearest and dearest, when his own flesh and blood did not believe in Him. Christ's feelings at this point in His ministry are quite sad and profound; *"I have become a stranger to my brothers, and an alien to my mother's children."* and again in John 7:5 it is also written, *"For even His brothers did not believe in Him."*

It's hard to fight against the flow isn't it? It's difficult to navigate and cross the consensus of opinion that may be against you. Misunderstandings of motives and intent will be rife at times like this. My goodness, even David the sweet singer of Israel, in all his littleness when talking openly about the greatness of God's almightiness, when having the audacity to suggest fighting Goliath of Gath by faith, had to suffer his first battle at the hands of his family; *"Now Eliab his oldest brother heard when he spoke to the men; and Eliab's anger was aroused against David, and he said, 'Why did you come down here? And with whom have you left those few sheep in the wilderness? I know your pride and the insolence of your heart, for you have come down to see the battle'." 1 Samuel 17:28.* Ha! It all could have ended there don't you think? Yes, it could all have ended right then and there!

It seems to me that trials of tremendous proportions come upon those that follow God against the flow. What differentiates those that turn back from the call of God on their lives, from those that pursue that call, despite suffering the lonely isolation of such enormous contra-flow pressure? Surely it has to do with that possession of the knowledge of the certainty of the joy that is set before us. We know God has told us to do this! We know God has told us to go there! We know God has told us to be this way! We know this fighting against the flow pleases Him and that makes us happy!

Keep swimming against the flow! Don't listen to those who with misunderstanding, lack of faith, and deep envy, are challenged and maybe even condemned in the highlighting of their own disobedience by your faithful obedience.

So, let me ask you today, do you have any measure of that certainty of joy that comes with knowing that He shall say to you, despite and because of the problems maybe, *"Well done my good and faithful servant?"* If so, then keep swimming against the flow! Don't listen to those who with misunderstanding, lack of faith, and deep envy, are challenged and maybe even condemned in the highlighting of their own disobedience by your splashing and a wiggling, jumping and a striding against the fearsome flow of a quiet conformity, a cultural conservatism, or a frolicking and rollicking, rocking revival, rooted in inauthenticity. Don't listen to them.

Listen: *"He went into the synagogue on the Sabbath day, and stood up to read. And He was handed the book of the prophet Isaiah. And when He had opened the book, He found the place where it was written: 'The Spirit of the LORD is upon Me, because He has anointed Me to preach the Gospel to the poor; He has sent Me to heal the broken hearted, to proclaim liberty to the captives And recovery of sight to the blind, to set at liberty those who are oppressed; to proclaim the acceptable year of the LORD.'" Luke 4:16-19*

Pray: Unless You go with me, and I know it, I dare not go and I cannot stand. Anoint me then, with the power of Your presence today. Amen!

Night-Whisper | **HEALING**

Dealing with damage

E very corporate company has in place plans for the backup and recovery of important client data. Disaster recovery as it is known, has been big business for many years. In addition to corporate disaster planning, in this is age of terrorism, every government and local authority also has plans to help recover from doom and destruction of every kind. The message is clear, plan for the worst and then live knowing that despite the cost, recovery is possible. However, though it may be wise, perpetually planning for and dealing with disaster is a stressful way to live. Don't you think?

2 Chronicles 24:2

And they hired masons and carpenters to repair the house of the LORD, and also those who worked in iron and bronze to restore the house of the LORD.
NKJV

All of us have or will encounter incidents in our life, which we count as personal disasters. One way or another we struggle on and to some measure we recover. To some measure, for I acknowledge that recover may be far too positive a word for some of us! The reason for that, is the scarring and damage that the disaster leaves both upon us and in us. Shakespeare puts it so well in "Sonnet 34", "Why didst thou promise such a beauteous day".

> *For no man well of such a salve can speak,*
> *That heals the wound, and cures not the disgrace:*
> *Nor can thy shame give physic to my grief;*
> *Though thou repent, yet I have still the loss:*
> *The offender's sorrow lends but weak relief*
> *To him that bears the strong offence's cross.*

Just how do you best deal with the damage then? May I suggest a few things?

First friends, we need to bow our knee to the Sovereign God and acknowledge that we are not in control. Our life is in His hands and we know that we cannot heal ourselves. We need His healing touch.

Secondly we need to face and feel the pain, acknowledge the loss and grieve over it. It's OK to feel and grieve you know! Indeed, it is an absolute necessity!

The wound can heal but the scar will stay. However, the choice regarding what we do with the scarring is ours?

Third, we need to acknowledge the difference between the wound and the scar. These are substantially different. Think about it. The wound hurts for a while, but the scarring is ugly and fixed upon us so much, that it is hard to forget. The scar has marked us and for better or for worse, it has changed us. We will never look the same again.

The wound can heal but the scar will stay. However, the choice regarding what we do with the scarring is ours? Shall these scars be perpetual reminders of our pain, or rather, will they become to us, our jewels of learning and growth, our red badge of courage, our sign of an overcoming sojourn.

Today I want to encourage you to live. Choose life, choose love, choose faith, choose hope. Live! Make your scars your very own war medals. Your purple hearts of conflict recovered from.

Listen: *"So I will restore to you the years that the swarming locust has eaten, the crawling locust, the consuming locust, and the chewing locust." Joel 2:25*

Hast thou no scar?
No hidden scar on foot, or side, or hand?
I hear thee sung as mighty in the land;
I hear them hail thy bright, ascendant star.
Hast thou no scar?

Hast thou no wound?
Yet I was wounded by the archers; spent,
Leaned Me against a tree to die; and rent
By ravening beasts that compassed Me, I swooned.
Hast thou no wound?

No wound? No scar?
Yet, as the Master shall the servant be,
And piercèd are the feet that follow Me.
But thine are whole; can he have followed far
Who hast no wound or scar?

Amy Carmichael – Irish Missionary to India for 55 years.

Pray: Father, if You will, come lift my scars and remove them completely. If not, then make beautiful and precious to me, in Jesus name I pray, amen.

Night-Whisper | **POWER**

Be a legend in your own lifetime

Sugar Ray Leonard is indeed an international sports legend. Born today in 1956, he learned to box aged 14 and it was family medical bills which forced him to enter the professional arena to help pay off mounting debts. He went on to win five world titles in five different weight categories, a record that stands to this day. Legend turned celebrity, Leonard has become like so many retired champions a motivational speaker and for fortune 500 companies, his most booked speech is on power. "Prepare, overcome, and win every round." Let's have a look at that today.

Joshua 1:11

"Pass through the camp and command the people, saying, 'Prepare provisions for yourselves, for within three days you will cross over this Jordan, to go in to possess the land which the LORD your God is giving you to possess'." NKJV

Preparation is important for overcoming. Preparation involves commitment, focus and sacrifice. If we do not prepare, we rarely overcome. *"For which of you, intending to build a tower, does not sit down first and count the cost, whether he has enough to finish it." Luke 14:28*

Overcoming, is a great link word in this little acronym of P.O.W.E.R! You see to overcome you don't just need to prepare, you need to continue in your preparation despite the many difficulties, disappointments and setbacks that will surely come upon you. In this fallen world, any attempt at improvement and progress will be thwarted by thorns and weeds of various kinds and any spiritual improvement, leading to possession of that which had previously been stolen from us, will be thoroughly resisted by the forces of darkness. Guaranteed! I have noticed that the powerful people of God are people of persistence and they are, by the blood of the Lamb, overcomers of every difficulty! Guaranteed!

The thorns never stop growing and the darkness only draws back to gather its forces and counter attack once more. The Kings highway winds its way through the valley of humiliation and up and along the frosty wind exposed crest of the hill of difficulty. There is a rest for the people of God, but it's when we pass through the gates dear friends, when we pass through those pearly gates! Until then, to ensure we arrive as champions in the courts of God, we need to make sure that we win every round! The point is this: objectives

Undaunted persistence will slowly, steadily, surely, gain you more and more ground

are often not achieved through overcoming but one difficulty or by winning just one battle. No, usually it's by winning many battles. Undaunted persistence will slowly, steadily, surely, gain you more and more ground, take you past the tipping point and move you into the glorious realm of being the trained and muscular overcomer, the prepared challenger, the seasoned champion, where you can stand atop your trod down thorns, your pulled up weeds, your slain giant and raise up it's severed head and shout: ***"I can do all things through Christ who strengthens me. All things! In all these things I am more than conquerors through Him who loved me." (Romans 8:37 & Philippians 4:13)***

So, just as preparation is the key to overcoming, so is persistent perseverance. We must plan, focus, and engage in such a way that we win every round. This should be our goal. As a note, I want to encourage you in your failure, because in reality, winning every round does not happen friends. Anywhere! Even Sugar Ray couldn't win every round! However, the focus is important and that is, to cultivate a no quarter, never give in kind of attitude.

Finally today, even if the final bell of this present fight you are in has gone and your all beat up and bloody on the canvas, then let me tell you friend, it's not time to give up! It's time to get back into training, and this time "Prepare, and Overcome and set your heart to Winning Every Round". All P.O.W.E.R. to you friend. All the power in heaven and earth. Now stop whining and start winning!

Listen: *"But you shall receive power when the Holy Spirit has come upon you; and you shall be witnesses to Me in Jerusalem, and in all Judea and Samaria, and to the end of the earth." Acts 1:8*

Pray: Lord, I am more than conqueror through Christ who loved me and gave Himself for me. Now Lord, help me live it every moment of every single day. Amen and amen!

Night-Whisper | **UNDERSTAND**

A triple whami without the fries

Bethesda was no longer worthy to see the wonderful works of God for Jesus cries out and says to them, "Woe to you, Chorazin! Woe to you, Bethsaida! For if the mighty works which were done in you had been done in Tyre and Sidon, they would have repented long ago in sackcloth and ashes." Matthew 11:21 So Jesus takes the blind man by the hand and leads him outside of the town of Bethsaida to perform this mighty work. Disbelief always leads to loss of wonder. Remember that.

Mark 8:23,24

So He took the blind man by the hand and led him out of the town. And when He had spit on his eyes and put His hands on him, He asked him if he saw anything. And he looked up and said, "I see men like trees, walking." NKJV

Maybe the blind man's eyes were all gummed up and kind of glued together? So, Jesus spits in His eye, allowing His spittle to ooze between the closed lids and not only to make the opening of the matted eyelids less painful but to also eek out some believing faith from the poor man's heart as well. Jesus always aids our required believing. For this particular blind man, with the outworking of the miracle, restriction and darkness were now replaced by space and light. Then Jesus calls out a testimony from him asking in effect, "How am I doing? How are you doing?" and He receives a most unusual answer? "I see men as trees walking?"

People who have been blind for some time, sensually speaking, no longer live in a space-time environment. They have lived for so long in just a time environment, that even when they regain their sight they are still spatially confused. Russell Grigg from the organization 'Answers in Genesis' says, "They have formerly been used to a world they accessed only by touch, hearing, taste, and smell and so tend to be baffled by *appearance* which, being optical, has no correlation in their other senses." You see, well I hope you do, that when a person can perceive the basic elements of a familiar object or experience, but then cannot recognize them, it is classified as a clinical condition which doctors call agnosia.

This condition takes a long time to correct, as often there is a need to develop new pathways in the visual cortex of the brain.

Friends, this man had received his sight! In the first part of the miracle, the organs of the eyes were now functioning correctly but the problem now was with his brain. Do you see that? Now look what the Master does. In another instant, Jesus performs another two miracles involving a radical change in both the blind man's neurological and psychological functioning, a change if you will in "the perceptual habits and strategies of a lifetime". Now that's amazing! Can you see this friends? The intertwining and interleaving of the delicate tissues of men, space and time have never been a problem for Jesus. The blind man is healed in his eyes, his brain and then in his psyche! Three miracles for the price of one! Yes sir, there are no lies, for here's a triple whami without the salted fries.

When a Christian spits in your face it can break your heart and wound your spirit but when God grabs your head and spits in your eye dear friend, I encourage you to get excited rather than offended

If you have ever wondered, how God could restore those blind years of your life, which the locusts have eaten? Well in our text, right here, right now, you can clearly see how He does it. Miraculously! When a Christian spits in your face it can break your heart and wound your spirit but when God grabs your head and spits in your eye dear friend, I encourage you to get excited rather than offended especially if you hear Him say to you, "Hey, how am I doin'? How are you doin'?" For nothing is impossible for the Lord.

Listen: *"Then He put His hands on his eyes again and made him look up. And he was restored and saw everyone clearly." Mark 8:25*

Pray: Lord, turn water into wine. Lord, get me to the other side in an instant. Lord, restore the years that the locust has eaten. Amen.

| Vol 02 | Q2 | NW00506 | May 19th |

The hour of power!

John wanted to be sure. Was he much like doubting Thomas? Interestingly we never here an account of 'doubting John' from our pulpits, therefore we need to ask, was John doubting here? Was he coming under tremendous spiritual pressure and beginning to doubt? Was he grieving for his near future knowing that the his ministry was coming to a close, "He must increase but I must decrease." Was John depressed and doubting or just doing his due diligence inn asking a final and very straightforward answer, "Are YOU the long expected, much awaited coming one?" Remember, John was prepared for his mission, knew his mission, had baptized Jesus and heard the stamp of the voice of God thunder over His life and seen God the Holy Spirit descend upon Jesus in the form of a dove. Did John doubt here? Or was He merely completing his 'due diligence?' I shall leave that with you, for my real focus tonight is how Jesus answered the question and it was not with a straightforward yes, but rather, with a an hour of unmitigated, unstoppable life changing feats of power.

Luke 7:20-23

When the men had come to Him, they said, "John the Baptist has sent us to You, saying, 'Are You the Coming One, or do we look for another?'" And that very hour He cured many of infirmities, afflictions, and evil spirits; and to many blind He gave sight. Jesus answered and said to them, "Go and tell John the things you have seen and heard: that the blind see, the lame walk, the lepers are cleansed, the deaf hear, the dead are raised, the poor have the gospel preached to them. And blessed is he who is not offended because of Me." NKJV

I have no doubt that Jesus loved John in a very special way. For me, the Bible text seems to actually drip with the honey of Jesus love, appreciation and respect for John. In addition, Christ also knew that John's departure from this world was at hand and that now, at the last, he would need something more than a simple verbal 'yes' to help him through the finish tape. Jesus is taking no oath here, where a simple 'yes' would be more than enough, (Matt

5:37) but rather, He is communicating in action the very veracity of His being, meaning and mission. He is communicating with the words and deeds of an hour of power.

Of course, I am not talking about a literal hour here, but the immediate response of Jesus to the question posed by John through his two disciples. Right there and then Jesus did one thing to four 'types' of people here.

He cured many of

- *Infirmities*
- *Afflictions and*
- *Evil Spirits*
- *And to many blind, He gave sight*

And He preached the Gospel to the poor declaring those who believe to be 'blessed' by God. Oh for sure, the lame walk, the lepers are cleansed, the deaf hear and the dead are raised, but these are simply the specific outworking's of the all-encompassing cure of infirmities, afflictions and evil spirits. In other words, Jesus did the specifics and a whole lot more as well. Indeed, Dr. Luke, at the end of his gospel account close by saying, "And there are also many other things that Jesus did, which if they were written one by one, I suppose that even the world itself could not contain the books that would be written. Amen. (John 21:25 NKJV) Look now though, for Jesus takes care to answer John's question in the present and with a fantastic display of an hour of power in the manifestation of 'Divine Therapeutic Medicine.' Indeed the word for cure is the word from which we get our English word, 'therapy.'

"And there are also many other things that Jesus did, which if they were written one by one, I suppose that even the world itself could not contain the books that would be written. Amen. (John 21:25 NKJV)

So, Jesus cured many of Infirmities. These are maladies that may also sometimes be reflected in m oral disabilities. These are sicknesses and diseases. Name a sickness, name a disease, yes, from cancer to venereal disease, Jesus cured the lot. (Matt 9:35) Some of these Infirmities, these diseases were directly devilish in origin and in temporal destination. So much so, that the New Testament hangs the word 'torments' onto the word 'disease,' sometimes referring to them as 'diseases and torments,' to indicate that some infirmities had taken people down to the very depths in there depraving destruction. Physically psychologically, financially, relationally, and spiritually, some of these diseases had taken people below the bottom. Jesus cured these people. None were beyond His healing power. His curing power. The diseases was made to depart, the depth of damage was instantaneously repaired, and the fraught and fractured disconnected person was left peaceful, whole, recovered and restored in every sense of the word. This was some range of curing friends, I mean it was fantastic! Disease and sickness and all there destructive connectivity was destroyed.

> *The diseases was made to depart, the depth of damage was instantaneously repaired, and the fraught and fractured disconnected person was left peaceful, whole, recovered and restored in every sense of the word.*

Jesus cured people of their physical afflictions, their 'plagues.' The idea is of a something that gives them a constant whipping! These physical afflictions were chronic, that is, continuing, persisting, never ending, unremitting and no doubt comorbid in manifestation, for you see, misery, even in physical affliction, always invites its mates to the never ending dung-fest of disease. So, the woman with a never ending emission of vaginal bleeding was healed by Jesus. Look now, long standing and comorbid afflictions can be instantly healed by Jesus. Where other doctors have failed and your finances have failed in finding a cure, one touch of Jesus fixes it all.

Jesus cast out 'Evil spirits,' even all manner of the disembodied spirits of the offspring of the fallen, (Genesis 6) and all spiritual co-morbid infestations of the same, were dealt with by Jesus. Demons always like to have their friends around. If they are going to 'squat,' then they rarely do it alone. Demons, evil spirits, physically manifest themselves in uncleanness of every kind, deceit, temptation, bondage, seduction, crippling infirmities, forced deafness, dumbness, feats of superhuman power and insight and limited future knowledge. These manifestations do not have their source in physical disease, but in spiritual demonization and oftentimes in actual, possession. These buggers need casting out. Let the angels of God deal with them once they are, in the name of Jesus, forced out of the physical.

This manifestation of Divine and Mighty Messianic power cannot be found in the fallen, the fraudsters the fake, or the technologically empowered. This all-encompassing instantaneous healing can only be found in the promised one, the awaited one, Jesus the Son of God. So, the two witnesses return to John and with wide eyes and excited lips no doubt recount to Him all they have both seen and heard. I believe John would have been satisfied, and in a state of mission completion, was now ready to move on.

> *This manifestation of Divine and Mighty Messianic power cannot be found in the fallen, the fraudsters the fake, or the technologically empowered.*

In closing may I encourage you to make good use of man's legitimate medicine. However, medicine does not cure everything, and mechanics does not make a man. Jesus, however, does completely cure and make whole once more. Therefore, and I say this with the greatest of respect, in accordance with the measure of your faith, make good use of Him.

The night is coming. Indeed, some of you reading this will no doubt be in that night. The mock miracles of past soulish sensationalism will not do. More than psychosomatic suggestion will be needed now, and the power of Christ needs to be made manifest for it is Him and His power which we now seek and rely upon.

Listen: *Later He appeared to the eleven as they sat at the table; and He rebuked their unbelief and hardness of heart, because they did not believe those who had seen Him after He had risen. And He said to them, " Go into all the world and preach the gospel to every creature. He who believes and is baptized will be saved; but he who does not believe will be condemned. And these signs will follow those who believe: In My name they will cast out demons; they will speak with new tongues; they will take up serpents; and if they drink anything deadly, it will by no means hurt them; they will lay hands on the sick, and they will recover." So then, after the Lord had spoken to them, He was received up into heaven, and sat down at the right hand of God. And they went out and preached everywhere, the Lord working with them and confirming the word through the accompanying signs. Amen. (Mark 16:14-20 NKJV)*

Pray: Look now my Lord. We question the veracity of some of these verses in Mark because we do not find them to be so. Oh we find the demons Lord, but not the power to cast them out. Oh we find the poison Lord, but not the cure to continue on. Oh we find the snakes, but cannot stop the slithering. Oh we find the sick, but Oh my God, we watch them die before us. Yes, all our disappointments Lord, we have covered with dispensationalism and other forms of self-excusing doctrine. Father, our faith is small, but now O Lord, the need for the true manifestations of the power of Your Son our Savior Jesus, must now be seen among and out of we Your saints. Lord, it must come like never before. In faith then, as we stand at the cusp of the end of all old things and the beginning of all things new, we cry with one voice together, "Where is the God of Elijah!" Lord, come and part the waters of our unbelief that we might return to the land of promises by the dry river bed-bottom testimony of Your present power. Amen and let it be so.

Night-Whisper | **PREPARE**

The Wine-boarding of the nations and a coming global 'dung-fest'

The infamous act of 'waterboarding' has been made famous worldwide as the primary tool of American torture. This is where water is poured over a cloth which is covering the face and airways of a bound and beaten prisoner, thus forcing the object of torture to experience the sensation of perpetual drowning. In our text for tonight, Jeremiah is told to 'Wineboard' all the reluctant and rebellious nations, to forcibly get them drunk and have them vomiting on the poured out wrath of the Lord. To those nations who refuse His terrible judgements, to those nations who refuse to voluntary drink the wine of His fury, God says "And it shall be, if they refuse to take the cup from your hand to drink, then you shall say to them, 'Thus says the Lord of hosts: "You shall certainly drink!"

Jeremiah 25:27-29

"Therefore you shall say to them, 'Thus says the Lord of hosts, the God of Israel: "Drink, be drunk, and vomit! Fall and rise no more, because of the sword which I will send among you."' And it shall be, if they refuse to take the cup from your hand to drink, then you shall say to them, 'Thus says the Lord of hosts: "You shall certainly drink! For behold, I begin to bring calamity on the city which is called by My name, and should you be utterly unpunished? You shall not be unpunished, for I will call for a sword on all the inhabitants of the earth," says the Lord of hosts.' NKJV

I, to my shame, when serving in the Royal Navy, have been many times drunk. Very drunk and vomiting. I have also witnessed other people very drunk and vomiting, and there is with this situation a complete and utter helplessness to those so thoroughly intoxicated. There is a tottering, a collapsing and a falling, followed by the passing out and unconscious immobilization of the binged up lunatic.

Read on from our text for tonight and you will find that when Jeremiah extends his 'wine-boarding' from Judah to the all the nations of the earth, that he switches from prose to poetry. Why? Well, they need to memorize and remember this most dreadful dirge It is as though God in starting to judge Jerusalem, and those nations around that now horrible hub of unhappy rebellion, finds that He cannot stop Himself in venting globally! Look now, for once judgement begins in the house of God, He cannot help but go on to do a clean sweep of all. Therefore, the Lion of Judah has now been awakened and while He is up and 'at 'em,' it is as though He says, "Well, now I'm up, riled and roaring, let's get the whole job done!" The roar of this Lion would now stir up an all-encompassing twister, a huge hurricane, a global catastrophic wind of judgement against every nation which God has legal contentions with concerning the breaking of His law, the murder of His saints and the rape of His grace. Death, destruction and desolation are the end products of this roaring storm which shall foam forth from the bare teethed mouth of the Lion of Judah. All the earths self-indulgent God rejecting 'rock and rolling' would now turn to nothing but rocking and reeling.

The message was clear, 'If the nations did not submit to God's judgements then He would have a global 'dung-fest.'

When Peter tried to protect Jesus from His being unlawfully arrested, the Lord said to him "Put up thy sword into the sheath: the cup which my Father hath given me, shall I not drink it?" (John 18:9 KJV) To drink the cup given by God then, is a symbol of submission to the very will of God. Jeremiah, the prophet to the nation's, had somehow communicated to each nation's ambassador the necessity to submit to God's judgements and be comparatively safe, secured, and somewhat preserved. or to rebel against God's judgments and with that be utterly destroyed. We do not know how he did this, and I have no time for 'perhapsing' tonight, (I shall leave a mass invitational banqueting picture with you) suffice to say, that Jeremiah communicated this action message well. The message was clear, 'If the nations did not submit to God's judgements then He would have a global 'dung-fest.' From it, those "Laid end to end, those killed in God's judgment that day will stretch from one end of the earth to the other. No tears will be shed and no burials conducted. The bodies will be left where they fall, like so much horse dung fertilizing the fields. (Jeremiah 25:33 from THE MESSAGE)

God will have clean clay pots to His glory, else He shall smash them all to pieces.

Church. Remnant. Let us put our own house in order. In this darkening night let us trust in the Lord with all of our heart and lean not on our own understanding. Let us in all our ways acknowledge His Lordship, love and care, His righteous acts and judgements, and have Him direct our paths by making 'right roads' rise up to meet us.

Let me be wrong, Oh God let me be so wrong. Let my cowardice and the smallness of size rightly brand me as nothing but a ' little chicken,' even a 'Chicken Little.'

Let me be wrong, Oh God let me be so wrong. Let my cowardice and the smallness of size rightly brand me as nothing but a 'little chicken,' even a 'Chicken Little.' Oh God let me have the embarrassment and shame of being wrong, for friends, this 'dung-fest' is coming and the wine-boarding is about to begin.

God's Kingdom must now begin to rightly manifest itself for the submission to God's will means the drinking of this cup. Therefore nations, drink this cup. Therefore remnant taste the bitterness of it. Now then Church, get ready, by all means and in every way, for that which is shortly to come upon us.

Listen: *"Therefore prophesy against them all these words, and say to them: 'The Lord will roar from on high, And utter His voice from His holy habitation; He will roar mightily against His fold. He will give a shout, as those who tread the grapes, Against all the inhabitants of the earth. 31 A noise will come to the ends of the earth — For the Lord has a controversy with the nations; He will plead His case with all flesh. He will give those who are wicked to the sword,' says the Lord."* *Thus says the Lord of hosts: "Behold, disaster shall go forth From nation to nation, And a great whirlwind shall be raised up From the farthest parts of the earth. "And at that day the slain of the Lord shall be from one end of the earth even to the other end of the earth. They shall not be lamented, or gathered, or buried; they shall become refuse on the ground. (Jeremiah 25:30-33 NKJV)*

Pray: Lord, why do the nations rage, and the people plot in vain against You? The kings of the earth set themselves, and the rulers take counsel together, against You the Lord and against Your Anointed Son our Savior Jesus , saying, "Let us break their bonds in pieces and cast away their cords from us." Yet, He who sits in the heavens shall laugh; You, yes, even You O

God shall hold them in derision. Then You shall speak to them in Your wrath, and distress them in Your deep displeasure: "Yet You have set Your King On Your holy hill of Zion saying to Him, "'You are My Son, today I have begotten You. Ask of Me, and I will give You the nations for Your inheritance, and the ends of the earth for Your possession." Therefore Lord Jesus, Loin of Judah, righteous judge, You shall break them with a rod of iron; You shall dash them to pieces like a potter's vessel. O God, give the leaders of this earth wisdom and let them be wise, and ready to learn. BE merciful to them and lead them to serve You O Lord with fear, and to rejoice with trembling. May they in relief, thankfulness and humility, kiss the Son, lest He be angry with them and they perish in the way, when Your wrath is kindled but a little. Blessed are all those who put their trust in You. O Lord, help me to put my trust in You. (adapted from Psalm 2).

Night-Whisper | **WITNESS**

Is that a feather?

Every seventeen years, billions of black shrimp-size bugs with transparent wings and beady red eyes, carpet trees, buildings, poles, and just about anything else that's upright, in a wide region of the US stretching from the eastern seaboard and west, through Indiana and then south to Tennessee. Though cicadas arrive every year, the enormity of this particular seventeen year emergence is known as "Brood X". The last one I remember was in 2004 and I still cannot get the smell out of that particular Kentucky summer out my nostrils, where thousands upon thousands of them, lay piled in small heaps, all dead and rotting, and still ringin in my ears is the nasty crunching of their dead carcasses cracking under my feet as I made my way to my car each morning. Then, there is the noise, oh my gosh, the constant rising and falling of the ever hot and buzzing noise! Yes, the cicada mating ritual produces a cacophony of courtship that can be heard through even the densest of suburban glass, making sure that in another seventeen years' time, they will arise to mate and die again in their thousands of millions, so that dogs, cats, fish, birds, squirrels, deer, raccoons, mice, ants, wasps and even some crazy human beings, may gorge themselves on these noisy, nasty and prolific little beasties.

Numbers 11:18-20

"Therefore the LORD will give you meat, and you shall eat. You shall eat, not one day, nor two days, nor five days, nor ten days, nor twenty days, but for a whole month, until it comes out of your nostrils and becomes loathsome to you, because you have despised the LORD who is among you, and have wept before Him, saying, "Why did we ever come up out of Egypt?"NKJV

With the overwhelming abundance of the seventeen-year cicadas, Brood X ensures their survival by satiating their predators within a few short days, thus leaving billions of them free to mate. By the end of June, all the Cicadas will have gone. Six to eight weeks after their departure the eggs that have been lain in the trees, will hatch, fall to the ground and eventually burrow into the earth and wait a further seventeen years until the reproduction of Brood X begins once again. What a cycle!

Friends, I need to tell you today that God knows how to fill nets with fish, baskets with overflowing bread, bottles with ever-pouring oil and pots of water with rich red wine. This is our Father's world and He has no problem in over production when He needs either to bless or to blast. Now, I wonder if in our lands of plenty, we might just consider that we in fact may be being blasted by God, especially as we observe the rising epidemic of obesity, diabetes, heart disease and the like? It's a thought worth considering.

This is our Father's world and He has no problem in over production when He needs either to bless or to blast..

I just might be right, for being born in 1960 I qualify (just) as being part of the generation-X brood and this brood of ours is still wandering in the desert having all we desire pour like green dismissive snot from our nostrils. There is nothing we do not want. There is nothing we do not have! Fatness, information, cynicism and a longing for some kind of Shangri-La called Egypt, are all ours in abundance. Peace, joy, satisfaction, family, community and the intimacy of the Almighty however, are what we truly need and what we truly, do not have.

Tell me friends, could it be possible that the present "Wal-Marting" of Christianity is the church simply catering to the consume and die mentality of the generation-X? I wonder if our reasons for shopping at super Wal-Marts are quite similar to the reasons we gen-Xers also go and shop at church? To gorge, consume, get fat and then die in judgement.

Oh Christian consumer, as you sit in the golf cart being ferried from the No10 parking lot towards the chandeliered entrance of your stadium sized, softly seated church and drop the kidz off in the Praize Factory and then take a few minutes to pop into the coffee shop, grab a Latte, kick your shoes off, stare at the indoor waterfall and occasionally glance at the man on the video screen in front of you and the thousands of others sat seated and staring at the oversized selection of jumbo-trons, hung like alien space invaders all over the tastefully decorated, user friendly inoffensive airspace, I wonder if you have ever considered such catered to, over-consumption as the judgement of God upon us?

Go on, look around you! There are no worries if you grab another Mocha and miss the message, for you can drop into the churches media center and pick up the little sermonette later, or better still, download the Godcast into your I-pod and listen to it tomorrow as you drive back to "Zion" with a number of the other Christianettes to see one of the army of paid staff counselors about, about, well about anything really! Anything that is except your sacrificial manned up service of the Most High God. Or maybe you can grab it the the next day when you come to the screening of the latest film of controversy in Youth Sanctuary No5, (old but nice) or Wednesday at the party for divorced moms meeting men or maybe even Thursday in the gym when you're

Next time we blow our nose, let's all check and see if there's any dead bird meat sat amongst the stickiness and try not to put it back into our mouth and suck on it as we skip along on our blind and fat little way

"spinning for Jesus" under the sweaty motivational guidance of one of the churches fitness coaches, or failing that, yes failing that, go on "fish fry Friday" out in parking lot No 11 adjacent to the new "worship celebration experience sanctuary", virtual cinema and "Holy Spirit" Shopping mall. Or maybe Saturday when it's time to satisfy your conscience cause you can't get to church on Sunday because you'll be down at the not so spectacular secular Mall doing some shopping for Christmas! Tell me fat boy, have you had a good look round recently?

Next time we blow our nose, let's all check and see if there's any dead bird meat sat amongst the stickiness and try not to put it back into our mouth and suck on it as we skip along on our blind and fat little way, singing along to the latest Christian CD's while ignoring the smell of our own rotting spirits deep in our souls and the sound of crumpling Christianettes crushed beneath our ever scampering little pigs feet, trotting all the way back to Egypt.

Yes indeed, it's all very distasteful, but hey, "not to us, but to the Lord be the glory, (sing with me now choir) not to us but to the Lord be the glory". Raise your hands to the jumbotron, clap with me and smile now, here we go, "not to us, but to the Lord be the glory,....."

"Just a minute," says our neighbor now staring at our nose, "Is that a feather?"

Listen: *"Look at the fig tree, and all the trees. When they are already budding, you see and know for yourselves that summer is now near. So you also, when you see these things happening, know that the kingdom of God is near. Assuredly, I say to you, this generation will by no means pass away till all things take place. Heaven and earth will pass away, but My words will by no means pass away." Luke 21:29-33*

Pray: Amen. Even so, come, Lord Jesus!

Night-Whisper | **HONOR**

The 'Pluck and Cut'

Just the other day I heard of yet another Pastor failing and falling into sin. This time it was not just one woman involved, but several, and not a few were in the congregation. This multiple adultery had apparently happened over many years. Meanwhile the church had grown in numbers, had completed an extensive building program and had gained an enviable reputation amongst the rest of the saints and their churches for being solid, steadfast, sure and blessed. All the while, the leader was committing adultery with many people. Darkness has an awful way of hiding itself in plain view. Indeed, one of the most awful attributes of sin is its mockery of God whilst it secretly expresses itself up close and personal. Jesus tonight, gets up close and very personal about this sin of adultery. He gets to the heart and the hand of the matter. Now then, before I go any further, if you are not going to be grown up about this, then I advise you to stop reading now.

Let me talk briefly about the Biblical preference of 'right' over 'left.' I say this because Jesus here focuses on the 'right' eye and the 'right' hand. Suffice to say, through all the 66 Books of the Bible, there is preference given to the right side of the body, in terms of the right side being atypical of spirit, honor, power, righteousness, provision, profit, pleasing, purity and direction.

Matthew 5:27-30

"You have heard that it was said to those of old, 'You shall not commit adultery.' But I say to you that whoever looks at a woman to lust for her has already committed adultery with her in his heart. If your right eye causes you to sin, pluck it out and cast it from you; for it is more profitable for you that one of your members perish, than for your whole body to be cast into hell. And if your right hand causes you to sin, cut it off and cast it from you; for it is more profitable for you that one of your members perish, than for your whole body to be cast into hell. NKJV

Jesus focus here is on the 'right' eye and the 'right' hand. Note first now, that the problem here is not with the object of our indulgence, but rather with the means of our indulgence. When our right eye, or our right hand becomes an animal snare to us, a trip line into a pit of destruction, a hole to stumble into headlong and whole, we must deal with means of the sinful indulgence rather than the object of our temptation. What a women wears, or rather, does not wear, might range from inappropriate to wantonly seductive, but remember, the issue is not the object, but rather, it is the means of our indulgence in the object. In other words, the sin and the solution to it, becomes our most thorough and personal responsibility.

Human law might say that adultery involves two people. God however, says one person and a fantasy is enough to break the law.

No of course, Jesus is using the term 'right hand' in a very general sense of every unrighteous action. However, the lust of the eyes leads to the self-pleasing of the hand, which in turn leads to the ultimate and illicit self-indulgence of that which is not ours. However, the reality of the sin, fostered initially by the indulgence the eye, first occurred within the adulterers heart. His mind became the secret bedroom of his fantasy, his hand, the initial means of that sinful expression, but it was his heart that indulged itself there. Suffice to say that even if the fantasy never became a reality, the sin of adultery was already a reality before God! Adultery had already been committed in his heart. Human law might say that adultery involves two people. God however, says one person and a fantasy is enough to break the law.

Jesus is not advocating amputation as a means to sanctification. Though in church history, many young men have cut their bells off to facilitate the latter, imagining that if their 'dong' had no 'ding-a-ling' that they would have no problem with lust. Such men were sorely disappointed. No , Jesus is not advocating amputation here, but rather, is using hyperbole to say that we must deal with the means of our indulgence of sinful lust. Yes, the root cause of this sin of adultery is lust, but Jesus says, "deal with the means of the indulgence of that lust." Do you get that? This side of heaven, sin will have its continual presence with us. Indeed, I might even suggest that we have still to be separated from the sinister left side of our being. (And please don't read too much into that!) I wonder if the Word is clear when it tells us that only death and heaven will separate us from the very presence of sin within us ,therefor, in terms of lust fulfilling itself in adultery, fill your right eye and your right hand with something else! Pluck out the focus of the lust and cut of the right hand of that indulgence. Jesus here is getting very practical.

If you have committed adultery in your heart, then there are three things to do.

Do not let the visual conduit of your eyes fuel the devil's playground of your mind.

First of all, confess you sin to God, repenting of the same and receiving the forgiveness he offers. Secondly STOP LOOKING. Do not let the visual conduit of your eyes fuel the devil's playground of your mind. Stop looking. Look elsewhere. Think about something else. Rejoice in your own wife of your youth.

Secondly, can I speak plainly here? Stop doing with all your might what your hand as previously found to do! The right hand fueling of sinful fantasy will make you spiritually blind and in being so, you will fall headlong into further sin. My fantastic friend, you are headed for disaster.

Thirdly, redecorate your mind. Think on pure things, think on right things, think on holy things, think on good things. Remove the dark curtains of your own self-indulgence and let in the light. It's time to pluck and cut.

In closing, may I say that if your adulterous fantasy has led to an adulterous reality, then you and your situation are an unexploded nuclear bomb and the defusing of this 'fat boy' will take time, wisdom, and the need for outside expertise. You need to go and see a same gender Pastor. You need to go and see a same gender counsellor. You need to start this process now.

Listen: *Dead flies putrefy the perfumer's ointment, And cause it to give off a foul odor; So does a little folly to one respected for wisdom and honor. A wise man's heart is at his right hand, But a fool's heart at his left. (Ecclesiastes 10:1-2 NKJV)*

Pray: Father, help me make my mind become the habitation of holiness, the playground lit by Your own pleasing smile. Help me find a spouse, and in the meantime or even in the longtime, a means to be holy without one. The O Lord, should You grant me this good thing, help me be their fantasy and they be mine in all their undying and un-denying fullness. Amen and let it be so.

Night-Whisper | **AUTHENTIC**

Cookie cut Christians

It was British Comedian Ken Dodd who I remember saying that "A husband is a man with the nerve taken out!" I think what he was alluding to is the much caricatured hen-pecked husband, you know, cowering and subservient, frightened to put a foot wrong, fearful to be wild. Now friends, in the same vein, it has been my observation that one of those horrible peculiarities that we in the Christian church seem to have is the tendency to produce "cookie cut Christians". Nice, neat, well-spoken, quiet, humble, obedient, polite people, cowering and subservient, frightened to put a foot wrong. I'm not knocking it (well maybe a little) but let's face it, some people had more life in them before they became Christians! Since that glorious day, it seems they have had their nerve removed.

1 Kings 1:13, 14

Go immediately to King David and say to him, "Did you not, my Lord, O king, swear to your maidservant, saying, 'Assuredly your son Solomon shall reign after me, and he shall sit on my throne?' Why then has Adonijah become king?" Then, while you are still talking there with the king, I also will come in after you and confirm your words.
NKJV

In the first book of Kings we are straight away presented with people who have been on the road a good wee while. Decrepit David, gnarly Nathan and old bent over Bathsheba are about to get the chop as Adonijah has just crowned himself king. A clear out is a coming and they are going to be thrown out with the garbage. Except that Nathan moves on the situation, managing the scene, both maneuvering the queen and manipulating the king. Nathan, the prophetic puppet master pulls all the right strings here. The result is simple, the kingdom is saved and Solomon becomes king instead of Adonijah. To round off the chapter, David, dear old man that he now is, gives command to his son concerning the dispatch of his enemies after his own forthcoming demise. Look! Can you see this? For one thing the people of the Bible are not, is nice and neat. There is little presented pretense. They are who they are, still red in tooth and claw.

My point is this. The Lord in the Scriptures reveals real people, in some raw and raging, ravaging situations. There is nothing placid, lame and cookie cut about them at all. They are not caricatures of the Christian life, they are people and it's all a bit messy and it's all a bit smelly.

Let's get the nerve back friends. Let's have the courage to be who we are in Jesus, who He created us to be; who He wants us to be.

Let's get the nerve back friends. Let's have the courage to be who we are in Jesus, who He created us to be; who He wants us to be. Let me ask you today, who are you? Do you know? Or have you had your nerve taken out as well? The other oven baked biscuits mightn't like you so much if you don't fit on the factory packet mind you. However, God and the world might find you that much more tasty. Some of you this morning, especially you men, simply need to go and get your nerve back!

Listen: *"And as the bridegroom rejoices over the bride, so shall your God rejoice over you." Isaiah 62:5b*

Pray: Lord, I am sorry that I am not the person I should be. Please help me to know how You delight in me. Help me to possess all that I am in You. Amen and Amen!

| Vol 02 | Q2 | NW00511 | May 24th |

Night-Whisper | **SEE**

Hearing the unspeakable

Imagine if you will, this consistent testimony that repeats itself in each new place which Paul arrives in when the Holy Spirit says to him "Man, you're getting in the neck here as well!" Imagine that. It's almost farcical isn't it? It makes Paul's mission almost akin to a black comedy. Eugene Peterson was right in paraphrasing Paul's comments in 1 Corinthians 4:9-10 : "It seems to me that God has put us who bear his message on stage in a theater in which no one wants to buy a ticket. We're something everyone stands around and stares at, like an accident in the street. We're the Messiah's misfits."

Acts 20:22, 23

And see, now I go bound in the spirit to Jerusalem, not knowing the things that will happen to me there, except that the Holy Spirit testifies in every city, saying that chains and tribulations await me. NKJV

Speaking of Messiah's misfits reminds me of one of my favorite lines from another black comedy, "Jacob the Liar," starring Robin Williams, which is set in a Jewish Ghetto in WWII. One of the characters remarks to a friend "I believe we are the chosen people, but I wish the Almighty had chosen somebody else!" Friends, I wonder if Paul ever felt like that? Humanly speaking of course, I would say, "Yes! Of course he must have." Yet the evidence of Paul's life and lip, appears to be contrary to that conclusion.

From the beginning, Paul knew that he would suffer for the name of Jesus Christ and he did: ***"In labours more abundant, in stripes above measure, in prisons more frequently, in deaths often. From the Jews five times I received forty stripes minus one. Three times I was beaten with rods; once I was stoned; three times I was shipwrecked; a night and a day I have been in the deep; in journeys often, in perils of waters, in perils of robbers, in perils of my own countrymen, in perils of the Gentiles, in perils in the city, in perils in the wilderness, in perils in the sea, in perils among false brethren; in weariness and toil, in sleeplessness often, in hunger and thirst, in fastings often, in cold and*** *nakedness - besides the other things, what comes upon me daily: my deep concern for all the churches."* 2 Corinthians 11:23-29.

So my question is this. What was it that stopped this man going insane with bitterness and indignation? May I suggest that nothing but a vision from God and of God, could sustain and empower such a commission? Maybe we should each seek a similar power infusing vision? So, how about it? Let me ask you today then dear friend; what is your driving vision? God! We need one don't we? What's your vision? Do you see it?

We're something everyone stands around and stares at, like an accident in the street. We're the Messiah's misfits."

Listen: *"I know a man in Christ who fourteen years ago - whether in the body I do not know, or whether out of the body I do not know, God knows - such a one was caught up to the third heaven. And I know such a man - whether in the body or out of the body I do not know, God knows - how he was caught up into Paradise and heard inexpressible words, which it is not lawful for a man to utter."* 2 Corinthians 12:2-4

Pray: O Lord, cover me and show me heaven. Unless You speak, unless You show, unless You manifest Your care and direction, the road ahead is far too steep and the deep, deep wood we have travelled into in Your great name, has become far too dark and far too cold for us to continue on without You. Speak Lord in the stillness whilst we wait on Thee, hushed our hearts to listen in expectancy. Amen.

Night-Whisper | **TRUST**

Dancing with diffidence

Now friends, she's often overlooked in the story. However, this morning I want to focus on her. Please God you will have read the Christian classic, *Pilgrims Progress* and know of Christian and Hopeful's little excursion off the Kings highway, into the grounds of Doubting Castle and Giant Despair. Here, they are kept locked up in a dungeon and are tortured by the giant. In this darkness, the giant Despair even suggests suicide as the only way out of the situation. Bunyan brilliantly portrays the felt hopelessness and torture of Christians who are in such a position. Fortunately, the word of promise, is the key discovered by Christian to be even in his heart, even and already in his very possession. This is the key that gets him, with great difficulty and danger, out of the dungeon, the castle and the grounds.

John 4:35-42

for He [God] Himself has said, I will not in any way fail you nor give you up nor leave you without support. [I will] not, [I will] not, [I will] not in any degree leave you helpless nor forsake nor let [you] down (relax My hold on you)! [Assuredly not!] AMP

Interestingly friends, in the story, giant despair never acts alone. Indeed, he is animated and directed by his unseen wife. Her name is Diffidence. She is the one who instigates the torture and directs the giant; Diffidence is the puppet master of giant Despair.

Webster defines diffidence as "shyness, lack of self-confidence, hesitancy". The hidden-ness of the character is the only action that matches this description. However, the roots of the word through middle English to Latin reveal the heart of diffidence and its true meaning which is distrustful! And there we have it. A word when said aloud even now still possesses the serpent's hiss. Disssssssssstrusssssssssful.

Don't dance with this diffidence friends. She is always tapping us on our shoulder, slurring her slippery suggestions into our hearts. "Did God really say?" "Look He's deserted you again." "Trust no one, not even God." "He takes care of them, but you? Ha! He obviously doesn't love you as much. Give Him the slip." "You are all alone now." And so she goes, on and on. Friends do not accept the kind and seemingly reasonable invitations of Miss Distrust! No, do not dance with Diffidence.

Listen: *"So we take comfort and are encouraged and confidently and boldly say, The Lord is my Helper; I will not be seized with alarm [I will not fear or dread or be terrified]. What can man do to me?" Hebrews 13:6 AMP*

Pray: So then Lord, let diffidence die in me. Let hope revive and reach to the very heavens even to Your great right hand. In Jesus name I ask it, amen.

Night-Whisper | **LIVE**

A large of whoooopass

A friend of mine once told me he thought he should have been born in Old Testament times, because then, you could really deal with your enemies instead of forgiving them, loving and praying for them. I know what he means, for New Testament Christianity is very demanding on the cheeks!

Psalm 139:21, 22

Do I not hate them, O LORD, who hate You? And do I not loathe those who rise up against You? I hate them with perfect hatred; I count them my enemies. NKJV

Our verses for today are not often spoken of in the church, whilst the following and last two verses of this particular psalm are often heard quoted. Here they are: **"Search me, O God, and know my heart; try me, and know my anxieties; and see if there is any wicked way in me, and lead me in the** way everlasting." They are nice, but so often they are utilized well outside of their original context.

Now friends, it is in fact quite easy to see why all these verses should appear together. As the old commentator, Adam Clarke puts it: "For he who hates, utterly hates, the practices of any man, is not far from hating the man himself. It is very difficult to hate the sin with all the heart and yet the sinner love." Opening a can of whooopass is a dangerous thing to do. Do you see that?

Remember that David was a man of extremities. He loved you or he hated you. It was all or nothing. There was no holding back with this man. You knew exactly where you stood with David; however, I suspect it made living with him a bit of a white-knuckle ride. Never-the-less, God seemed to love him dearly and David was at least a little aware of the problems associated with his passion. In other words, he knew that "you don't open 'a large can of whooopass' without getting some of it on yourself." If I might paraphrase him he says, "These passions overwhelm me. There they are, I cannot deny them and I must express them. Never –

the-less I know what is in me, so search me and know me and remove the root of my own wickedness."

I like that. It's dangerous stuff mind you isn't it? Imagine if the church or your place of work suddenly had members and employees really expressing how they felt about things, people and issues. The volcanic eruption doesn't bear thinking about does it?! I can't help but wonder though, if it is possibly a healthier way to live?

"For he who hates, utterly hates, the practices of any man, is not far from hating the man himself. It is very difficult to hate the sin with all the heart and yet the sinner love. ".

I am sure we need to learn how to express ourselves without sinning. You will notice I did not say hurting, offending, upsetting, or rocking the boat. Nope. It does not happen like that. Emotional expression can be a wild wave to ride. So, today friends, very carefully and without sinning, why not go on and express yourself. Do some wild dancing! But please weigh down your linen ephod, put some underpants on and open any large cans of whooopass with the greatest of self-examining care!

Listen: *"Then David danced before the LORD with all his might; and David was wearing a linen ephod." 2 Samuel 6:14*

Pray: Lord, help me to live before You in extravagant passion. Search me and show me my sin. Let me own it and then willingly forsake it today and as I twirl before You, may all my poisonous emotions drip from my fingertips and Lord my Lord, will You fill me with Your extravagant joy! In Jesus name I pray, amen.

Night-Whisper | **COURAGE**

Sissies or soldiers?

In America I am sure that my Southern friends will forgive me this morning for referring to the birth today of a most famous daughter of America in 1819, Mrs. Julia Ward Howe. Anti-slavery activist, suffragette, and Unitarian, I might not agree with all of her theology or her politics but the poem she penned on visiting the Union Army of the Potomac is inspiring. To the tune of "John Browns Body", the "Battle Hymn of the Republic" became the marching song of the Union army and an inspiration to countless millions. Though the first three stanzas are marvelous, the last two stanzas surpass them all when they say:

Psalm 58:6-8

O God, break off their fangs. Tear out the teeth of these young lions, Lord. Let them disappear like water into thirsty ground. Make their weapons useless in their hands. Let them be as snails that dissolve into slime and as those who die at birth, who never see the sun. TLB

He has sounded forth the trumpet that shall never call retreat
He is sifting out the hearts of men before His judgment-seat
Oh, be swift, my soul, to answer Him! be jubilant, my feet!
Our God is marching on.

In the beauty of the lilies Christ was born across the sea,
With a glory in His bosom that transfigures you and me:
As He died to make men holy, let us die to make men free,
While God is marching on.

I have been witness in my lifetime to some of the greatest new worship songs I have ever heard. They move me from earth to heaven in prostrate adoration and so they should, for He is worthy. However friends, amongst all this glorious worship, the church militant seems to have laid down its weapons, seems to have retired from the field before the final battle, seems to have failed to finish off the enemy, cut the head from Goliath and stamp the serpent thoroughly under its feet. Friends, look you. In all our "new worship experience," where are the war songs of the mighty men of God the All-mighty? Where are the fierce lion like men of the greater David? Where are the great hearts of this day? Who will break the enemy ranks and draw water from the well of Bethlehem for King Jesus today? Are all we have in our ranks today, simply sissies with a dream? History maker fakers? Surely not? What about you? Are you a song singer or a real history maker? Faker of maker? What are you today?

Stop singing like a sissie man! Enough of this hold me, stroke me, feel me, touch my hair and tell me that you love me rubbish!

Stop singing like a sissie man! Enough of this hold me, stroke me, feel me, touch my hair and tell me that you love me rubbish! For God's sake! for His Kingdom's sake! Grow up man, get up, and go up to some mountain and take it for Jesus, take it with Jesus, take it because of Jesus. Stop the singing and start the soldiering, maybe then you'll have something to sing about. In the meantime I wonder if God is simply saying, "Just shut up!"

Rise up O Men of God, have done with lesser things give heart and soul and mind to God to serve the King of Kings!

Listen: *"For You have armed me with strength for the battle; you have subdued under me those who rose up against me. You have also given me the necks of my enemies, so that I destroyed those who hated me." Psalm 18:39-40*

Pray: Teach my hands to make war, make my arms strong to bend the bow of bronze, grant me the shield of Your salvation, and Your right hand to uphold me. By Your gentleness, make me great. Enlarge my path beneath my feet that I might not slip up in the pursuance of my enemies, until each one is overtaken and thoroughly destroyed by both Thee and me! Amen.

Night-Whisper | **HONOR**

Humane humanity?

In Germany between 1942 and 1943 as many as 20,000 people fell to this particular form of political execution used by the Nazis. Hitler considered it to be a most demeaning way to be dispatched. Indeed, more people were killed using this method in Germany than during its use in revolutionary France and interestingly, it was last used in Europe as recently as 1977!

Genesis 9:5,6

Surely for your lifeblood I will demand a reckoning; from the hand of every beast I will require it, and from the hand of man. From the hand of every man's brother I will require the life of man. "Whoever sheds man's blood, by man his blood shall be shed; for in the image of God He made man." NKJV

The family whose name became associated with this instrument of death, (though it was not a new invention) begged the French government to change the name of the machine. When they refused to call the instrument of death something else, in great shame, the family changed their own name! The French doctor who is attributed with its invention was in fact against capital punishment and instigated the design to more humanly dispatch the guilty and the condemned. Joseph Ignace Guillotine, was born today in 1738.

I have no wish to fuel the fires of the controversy of capital punishment. No, let the Word speak for itself. However, no matter which side of the argument you may be on, I do wish to encourage you today regarding the great encouragement contained in these particular Bible verses. At the very least we can say this; that God puts an enormous value on human life, on human blood. Friends, God's most used color in the painting of pictures is the color red. Red gets our attention you see, for the color red is a flying flag of danger and destruction, of devastation and death. David says God takes note of each tear that is shed and everyone is kept in His bottle and so in light of that alone, I can tell you today that

God takes note of every drop of blood that is shed as well! Each red drip, dropped unjustly into the hungry ground, cries loudly to its creator for justice and one day, it shall receive its desire for revenge and retribution as everyone gives an account for the mauling and marking of the image of the Maker.

God takes note of every drop of blood that is shed.

You are the image of God! Don't forget it. Honor one another for this at least, even, for this alone. For we all bear the "Imageo Deo". Every single one of us. You shall not murder!

Finally today, may I point out that many of our cities now have an abortion rate which is higher than the birth rate and the screaming, red blood prayers of the millions of unborn cry out for vengeance against us. Do you honestly believe that God will not avenge such a carnage and such a desecration of His image? The silence of the church against such genocide is a pox on our face of worship. The inactivity of the church against such mass murder makes us as complicit and as guilty as all the neighbors of Auschwitz. Think about that today.

You shall not murder.

Listen: *"What have you done? The voice of your brother's blood cries out to Me from the ground." Genesis 4:10-11*

Pray: Lord, give us clean hands, give us clean hearts, let us not lift our souls to another.

Night-Whisper | **FIGHT**

Scars, wounds and war-horses

The Christian's call to arms is a difficult subject friends. However, it is somewhat easier when we recognize that though the weapons of our warfare are not carnal, they are never the less mighty in God. (2 Cor 10:4, 5) We walk a challenging path and many times pure pacifism is not the right option. It certainly is not the option in the spiritual realm!

Revelation 6:9,10

When He opened the fifth seal, I saw under the altar the souls of those who had been slain for the Word of God and for the testimony which they held. And they cried with a loud voice, saying, "How long, O Lord, holy and true, until You judge and avenge our blood on those who dwell on the earth?" NKJV

Yet how can we peacemaker sons of the Most High, love fiercely and then engage in warfare at the same time? How can we be the ministers of both life and death? How can we express goodness towards our enemies and then have victorious greatness over them at the same time? How can we have voice and conquest? How can we have anger and embracing? How can we ferociously fight without falling into sin? Of course it's difficult and of course it's dangerous for Christians to engage in warfare! However, maybe we should expect to experience more of both this particular difficulty and danger than we do?

We live on an enormous battleground. The church *is* militant, *is* fighting, and *is* suffering victory and loss all along its forceful front. The shedding of tears and blood is evident in both present victory and defeat. Of course it is, for we are not yet home. I wonder then, if some of us will be greatly embarrassed at the judgment seat of Christ when we are asked to roll up our sleeves before the Commander to all heavens armies and all the watching host! Will He look at them and us and repeat these lines:

Hast thou no scar?
No hidden scar on foot, or side, or hand?
I hear thee sung as mighty in the land,

I hear them hail thy bright ascendant star,
Hast thou no scar?

Hast thou no wound?
Yet I was wounded by the archers, spent,
Leaned Me against a tree to die; and rent
By ravening beasts that compassed Me, I swooned:
Hast thou no wound?

No wound, no scar?
Yet, as the Master shall the servant be,
And, pierced are the feet that follow Me;
But thine are whole: can he have followed far
Who has no wounds nor scar?

Amy Carmichael

Maybe Job was right, that unlike most of us Christians, it is only prepared war-horses that can sniff the battle from afar, for only they are girded with strength and clothed with thunder from on high. (Job 39:19-25) Maybe I'm not thinking right friends but let me ask some of you today, some of you up for a fight, some of you frustrated at simply shining pews with your Sunday morning pants, some of you men who may be agitated in the slips, waiting and ready for action: "Do you hear the sound of trumpets calling? Are the hairs on the back of your neck raised and your arms ready for action in the service of your King today?" If so, then maybe you are a war-horse of the Lord and frankly, though you might frighten some of the old mares, you never-the-less need to go out and look for a fight. He who has ears to hear, let him hear and he who has nostrils, let him sniff!

> *Maybe you are a war-horse of the Lord and frankly, though you might frighten some of the old mares, you never-the-less need to go out and look for a fight.*

Listen: *"He mocks at fear, and is not frightened; Nor does he turn back from the sword. The quiver rattles against him, the glittering spear and javelin. He devours the distance with fierceness and rage; Nor does he come to a halt because the trumpet has sounded. At the blast of the trumpet he says, 'Aha!' He smells the battle from afar, the thunder of captains and shouting." (Job 39:19-25)*

Pray: Master. You came and brought a sword. You came to preach peace and to wage war. You came to unite and to divide. Lord help me, and keep me in Your holy boundaries, but Oh God don't let me rust out. No Lord, please let me bust out! In Jesus name I pray, amen!

Night-Whisper | **COURAGE**

Political pyres and the cleansing of leprosy

In France, high above the Vienne River, stands the remains of the fortified castle of Chinon. A few years ago, I stood on the supposed exact spot where Joan of Arc picked out Charles VII, the French Dauphin (heir to the throne and whom Joan had never seen before) who was himself, hidden by disguise within the French Royal Court, to test her famed mystical acumen.

1 Kings 8:17

Then it happened, when Ahab saw Elijah, that Ahab said to him, "Is that you, O troubler of Israel?"NKJV

The English, who for years laid claim to the territories of France, had once again invaded that fair land and were now, via the Duke of Salisbury, laying siege to Orleons, the last stronghold before the fall of the Dauphin's remaining territory. Joan, at Chinon, having picked out the Dauphin, shared with him a prophecy that had been revealed to her regarding his rightful claim to the throne. Noting that the Dauphin's own mother had already deserted to the English, thereby declaring her own son's illegitimacy to the throne, the arrival of Joan's seemingly 'prophetic' words and revelations were said to make the besieged Dauphins face radiant!

Consequently, Charles VII sent this peasant girl mystic to Poitiers, where after three weeks of theological questioning, the clergy declared her to be both orthodox and called to lead the French army. A verified saint, now at the head of the army, brought both reform and recruitment to the French ranks. Joan's leadership (aged just 15 remember!) lifted the siege of Orleons and turned the tide for the French, allowing the Dauphin to be crowned King.

Politics and lack of needful provision from the throne mark the rest of Joan's life. Eventually she was betrayed into the hands of the English, who, it is believed out of revenge, charged her with witchcraft and the crime of cross dressing, for which she was burned at the stake today in

1431 in Rouen, at the exact same place her beloved Dauphin had been crowned King of France.

Voices from heaven, a board of theologians and the King himself all vouchsafed her divine mission, yet what an end? Friends, we can at least see and apply this principle: that neither miracles nor the machinations of the metaphysical can keep anyone from ultimate harm. I don't know what Joan was but I know that politics has always betrayed the prophetic and always will, for one is rooted in the spiritual domain whose source is Jesus, whilst the other is rooted in the worldly domain whose source too often, is right from the bosom of the evil one. Sometimes I wonder if politics is a disease rather than a calling?

Political disease when practiced amongst the body of Christ spreads it's same killing spores across the prophetic, leaving the church both politically correct but most pitifully pathetic.

This same political disease when practiced amongst the body of Christ spreads it's same killing spores across the prophetic, leaving the church both politically correct but most pitifully pathetic. Church politics is a leprosy, the cleansing of which will mean the burning of the whole house.

I have a simple message for you today: If you find yourself playing politics in the church or even at work, then beware friends, because there's probably fire at the end of it all. Fire!

Listen: *"Therefore the wisdom of God also said, 'I will send them prophets and apostles, and some of them they will kill and persecute,' that the blood of all the prophets which was shed from the foundation of the world may be required of this generation, from the blood of Abel to the blood of Zechariah who perished between the altar and the temple. Yes, I say to you, it shall be required of this generation." Luke 11:49-51*

Pray: Lord. Help me today in my dealings with others, to move in the powerfully prophetic and not the politically pathetic. Lord, save Your church from the cleansing burning of political leprosy. Amen and let it be so.

Night-Whisper | **KNOW**

Intriguing intercourse and God's mates amongst the masses

B ible reading can just get so monotonous and boring can't it? Don't get me wrong, I have found it to be the most exciting book in the world and believe it to be the very Word of God. However, some days and they are far too frequent, it's just another tick in my box of important spiritual exercises to complete. The Bible often becomes as dry and as palatable as old toast! What's the problem here? Well maybe Tozer in his book *The Pursuit of God* puts his finger right on it yet again! This is what he says: "The modern Scientist has lost God amidst the wonders of His world; we Christians are in real danger of losing God amidst the wonders of His Word. We have almost forgotten that God is a person, and as such can be cultivated as any person can. It is inherent in personality to be able to know other personalities, but full knowledge of one personality by another cannot be achieved in one encounter. It is only after long and loving mental intercourse that the full possibilities of both can be explored." I would only add that God is interested in more than mental intercourse friends, for He plays on the field of full and total social interaction. Every Biblical personage will truly tell you that God wants to know you and for you to know Him and of course, I speak in the full Biblical understanding of the word know!

Genesis 22:12

"Do not lay your hand on the lad, or do anything to him; for now I know that you fear God, since you have not withheld your son, your only son, from Me."
NKJV

God is not interested in how many chapters you have ploughed through today. He is not interested in your religious observances or your spiritual exercises. Maybe the dry toast nature of these things is making Him both bored and sick as well! He wants more. Consider this; God might just find you intriguing! The all-knowing God may want to so prod and probe the depths of your being just for the sole purpose of the excitement the delight and maybe even the disappointment sometimes, of simply getting to know you experientially. Have you considered this?

That you, are worth knowing. Maybe God invites you to do the same. You know? To find Him in person, to be so intrigued by Him that today you will set sail on the sea of the infinite and find Him to have been there all the time, even at your very elbow.

God, me thinks, has His mates among the masses and these are the people who have taken the time to unfold their hearts to Him, and Him to them.

Vast and deep, He is by your side dear Christian, waiting to be discovered all the more. God, me thinks, has His mates among the masses and these are the people who have taken the time to unfold their hearts to Him, and Him to them. Yes, they know one another and are glad.

One day in the long ago, God poked Abraham and asked him to kill his son, his only son, whom he loved. When Abraham went to do this, God in fact stopped him, but in the stopping of this action already completed in the heart of Abraham, God declared, "Now I know!" God experienced a knowledge that He had not experienced before. "Now I know!" I tell you, head knowledge is great, but experiential knowledge is better. Now tell me, when was the last time you poked God and said, "Ahem, excuse me but…?" I suspect that God would like our payers to be part of our spiritual formation and that our spiritual formation is to be like Christ, fully knowing the Father. The knowledge of God, is intriguing intercourse, intimate, inexhaustible, infinitely joyful. It is most certainly better, than dry old toast.

Listen: *"And this is eternal life, that they may know You, the only true God, and Jesus Christ whom You have sent." John 17:3*

Pray: Father, let us begin today to know one another in fresh, fruitful and ever exciting opportunities. "Ahem, excuse me Lord but why, who, what, when, where and why?" Jesus, please begin a never-ending conversation with me today, "Ahem!" and amen!

Night-Whisper | **CHOOSE**

Mouthy malice and how to shut the little creep right up!

I don't know if it's still there but the graffiti sprayed across a bridge as you drove up the M1 in England towards the city of Luton always grabbed my attention. In desperate scrawl it read "A Town Called Malice," a direct reference to a song by the 1980s group, The Jam.

Ephesians 4:31

Let all bitterness, wrath, anger, clamour, and evil speaking be put away from you, with all malice.NKJV

Paul Weller penned some incredible words to this song, which was later used as part of the soundtrack in the film *Billy Elliot*. I suppose being British and originating from that part of British social structure the lyrics, the location, and the spirit of the song all echo deep in my being. Here's the opening lines:

Better stop dreaming of the quiet life –
Cos it's the one we'll never know,-
And quit running for that runaway bus –
Cos those rosey days are few-And –
Stop apologizing for the things you've never done,-
Cos time is short and life is cruel –
But it's up to us to change
This town called malice.

I am acquainted with malice. Pastorally I have seen it to be that which is most manifest in the hurt, the rejected and the robbed. Personally, malice is always my most unwelcome yet very welcome justifying minister and mentor, even tormentor. We all have a strange love-hate relationship with malice. You know what I mean. Yes, I think you do.

The sin of malice is insidious to humanity. It is linked directly to the proud house of sinful self. Malice clings to you like old gas, passed from the cabbage you ate yesterday or like malevolent misery, it sits astride your mouth and stretches your cheeks downwards in fearful weighted frowning. Malice manipulates the mind, has menace as its cousin and murder as its twin. Malice is hate incarnate. Malice is dear friends, nothing but dark, murky and malevolent sin. Yet we so often quietly welcome it through the back door of our heart, late at night, when all the good neighbors are asleep.

Yes, malice is very vocal in justifying its existence. After all, "Didn't they…" and "If he hadn't…" and "Except for…" and "I was only…".

Malice is a particularly tricky form of sin. For once welcomed into our hearts, it can morph itself into seeming light and righteousness. Yes, malice is very vocal in justifying its existence. After all, "Didn't they…" and "If he hadn't…" and "Except for…" and "I was only…"

Yet what a mad mouthed, self-justifying monster, malice can morph into! For malice cannot be reasoned with once it has been justified. It is too powerful. I would suggest that neither can it be fought against and overcome! For if you try and attack it, malice will only get stronger! Rather then , malice is to be dealt with in a most disdainful way. Yes, like a child with an old toy, we must continually lay it aside. I mean persistently and continually ignore it! This will offend it, but I tell you friends, it will eventually shame it, quieten it, defeat it and suck the self-justifying and sour little life out of it. Make no mistake though; the process must be a continual and disdainful laying aside.

Finally, and best of all, malice must be ignored. Mostly this is best done by taking up some new and righteous toy, even some better friend. If malice is in your house, ignore it with practical intent. So child of God, today if your meal is mouthy malice, then why not lay the losing louse aside and start playing with the some of the better toys of the Kingdom. Yes , if you do both these things, that is, disdain it and ignore it, then eventually, malice will leave of its own accord, slinking out of the back door late at night into the foggy darkness, disgusted and hurt. It wont even slam the door. Try it and see if I am correct for it's up to us to change this town called malice and I tell you, this is just the way to do it!

Listen: *"And be kind to one another, tender hearted, forgiving one another, even as God in Christ forgave you." Ephesians 4:32*

Pray: Loving God, help me today, to lay death aside and pick up life! In Jesus name I pray, amen!

Night-Whisper | **FIGHT**

Of midnight street cleaners and mocking the mad dogs of the night

How did you sleep last night? Did their howling keep you awake? Did you hear their padded paws prowling up and down, up and down, or their scratching and clawing at the door of your heart. Listen to the opening words of this poem, entitled the "Boo Radley Blues":

My blues are dressed in the palest of white
My blues only come out in the deep dark of my night
When quietness falls and all is so still
When weak the wall of this my will
To hold this skulking, sulking Boo Radley
Of my heart
Of my heart.

Psalm 59:14,15

And at evening they return, they growl like a dog, and go all around the city. They wander up and down for food, and howl if they are not satisfied. NKJV

Sometimes, many of us do not see the night as a gift for His beloved sleep but in trepidation, we perceive in the darkness, the open gate of an eerie silence which will eventually let loose the scary scavengers of accusation and condemnation, of regret and hatred into our minds, so as to both hound and worry us once more. For many people, the night holds little comfort.

Remember dear ones that these relentless mad dogs of the night are pack animals and they rarely scavenge alone, that is the why the night can bring a multitude of condemning woes, of frightful and ripping accusations. These mad dogs of the night appear so uncontrollable and we to be so indefensible against them, that many of us have even taken to pills or alcohol, to try to keep these mad, bad dogs of the night away. But they will not go for you see, the garbage in the streets of our city is too much of a temptation for them. Yes, garbage in our streets. Now that's the real problem.

So how can we, the temporarily insane, for that is how we feel, yes, how can we, who are hounded almost to death by accusation, regret, condemnation, self-annihilation, and soulish degradation, how can we then live well and live somewhat peaceful in the day, whilst we are being so troubled and confounded, defeated and desperately hounded by these mad dogs of the night, that even steal away His beloved gift of sleep? How can we rid our midnight streets of such a howling?

It is the hardest thing in the world to do but we must have faith in the goodness, grace, forgiveness and power of God toward us. Calling for such effort of belief and trust when all you want to do is crawl under a rock and die is I know, both a terrible and a trying demand! Yet no matter how hard it be, we must make take this hike of the Holy hypocrite, for friends, this is good hypocrisy. (Yes, there is such a thing.) Allow me to tell you more.

You see, this hike of the holy hypocrite is a hypocrisy that verges on madness, for when we acknowledge our desperate state, we must then also begin to sing to our desperate state! Yes! When a crack appears in the clouds friends, sing. When a feather of hope falls on your cheek, sing. When a faint breeze of brightness passes you by, sing. Curse and rage if you must and when you must but when a glimmer of hope flickers somewhere in the corner of your eye, take the brief opportunity of distraction that it avails to you, then turn your head to it and sing. It's madness I know. Yet what have you to lose? Dogs hate singing. Sing at midnight when you can but always, I mean always sing in the sunshine.

Go on try it. Mock these mad dogs of the night by singing of His might, both through the day and especially through the night.

Go on try it. Mock these mad dogs of the night by singing of His might, both through the day and especially through the night. If you do, these terrible dogs of discomfort, will slowly but eventually draw back and when evening comes, they shall not return!

Now, when this is done, when the howling stops, then my friend, it's time to clean your streets. Big job! Long job! Permanent job! And the instruction of how to do it well is another story for another day, but for this day, please remember: Have faith, take faith, and sing to the mad dogs of the night, sing to them about Him and His great love for you.

Listen: *"But I will sing of Your power; yes, I will sing aloud of Your mercy in the morning; for You have been my defense and refuge in the day of my trouble. To You, O my Strength, I will sing praises; for God is my defense, my God of mercy." Psalm 59:16-17*

Pray: Teach me O Lord, the song of the madman. Teach me to sing, in the face of my accusers, even in the face of the dreadful and dogged, night black enemies of my soul. Then O Lord, help me keep my streets clean. In Jesus name I ask it, amen.

Night-Whisper | **CULTIVATE**

The great British bustard

Able to stand to the height of an adult roe deer, they can also be more than a meter long and weigh up to 15kg! They were last seen in Britain during the 1830s, however, because of it's delicious and succulent meat, it was sought after by the nations then top chefs in such massive proportions, that the great bustard was hunted to extinction in that fair and sceptered isle!

Proverbs 18:24a

A man who has friends must himself be friendly.NKJV

At the beginning of this new century, from some 40,000 birds still left in parts of Europe, the world's heaviest flying bird, the "crown of British bio-diversity" is being re-introduced to mainland Britain by the "British Great Bustard Group".

So what? Well two words come to mind friends. Consume and cultivate. You see the problem with the great bustard is that they were consumed without cultivation. If you want a thing to last, you need to cultivate it and remember, this applies to just about everything in life. After all, once you've licked your last stamp you can't post your latest letter! See what I mean?

In so many marriages, the last stamp was licked long ago. Love has been so consumed from the now empty person, so relied on, so taken for granted, that in the end, they have no more to give. They are all loved out. The main problem is that the marriage has not been cultivated. The same problem can be manifest in any relationship and especially friendship. This lost jewel of Christian community, true soul friendship, is also a two way street you see. It too must be cultivated.

Now listen, doesn't it follow then, that your relationship with Christ must run the same course? Be cultivated and not just not consumed? So, if your prayer life is merely a shopping list, if every time you look to heaven and all your doing is holding a card from the community chest, if all your religious activity is merely "covering the bases" lest you or a loved one gets stepped on, then may I suggest, you are a consumer and not a cultivator! Change today. Get in on the business of cultivation. Begin a romance with Jesus. He's been faithful. He's stuck close when you have not. Stop just consuming and start cultivating. Turn to Him today. Court Jesus and maybe, just maybe, you might catch Him if you can!

Listen: *"There is a friend who sticks closer than a brother." Proverbs 18:24.*

Pray: Faithful God. Lovely Jesus. Stick closer to me than any brother, for my heart is prone to wander and fearful in its forgetfulness. Teach me how to faithfully cultivate and not just to consume. Lord, how may I cultivate our relationship then? Show me Lord please, in Your great name I pray, amen.

Night-Whisper | **CONSIDER**

Naked and not ashamed

It was a very Southern wedding. The preacher, even without his cowboy hat, looked like an extra from *Bonanza* of long ago. He gently chided the groom and publicly threatened him with a none too pastoral visit in the future, should he not take care of his new beautiful bride. The pastor was nicely threatening. Yet there was no doubt about it, he was threatening! There was intent in his voice. This pastor had seen them both grow up and loved them both dearly. He knew of their virginity and boasted of it publicly. It was a very Southern wedding. I loved it.

Psalm 27:4

One thing I have desired of the LORD, that will I seek: that I may dwell in the house of the LORD all the days of my life, to behold the beauty of the LORD. NKJV

The nearest town to the village I grew up in is called Chesterfield and it is in Derbyshire. God's country! The nickname of its soccer team is the "Spirites." This is because although St Mary's may be the largest church in Derbyshire, it is most famous for its enormous and very crooked spire. Historians have wondered that if in the 14th century, at the time the spire was being built, the onset of the Black Death in Chesterfield may have killed many skilled craftsmen, such that, maybe the less skilled survivors, used too much green timber in the spire, which, on drying out, bent the steeple or that maybe the badly calculated construction just simply could not hold the weight of it all and so quite simply, it became bent and twisted? Local people of course have their own explanation. Rumor had it that a virgin was getting married at the church one day and the spire, never having seen a virgin bride before or since, turned and leaned over to get a closer look. Legend now says that, "Should such a virginal event ever happen again, the spire will think it commonplace and straighten up again." It hasn't happened yet!

At the very Southern wedding, the virgin bride and groom were beautiful. It is not crude to suggest, that the groom longed to look on the nakedness of his wife on their wedding night. Indeed, John Eldridge in his book *Wild at Heart* quotes William Blake saying, "The naked woman's body is a portion of eternity too great for the eye of man." Eldridge suggests that the naked beauty of a woman is God's finishing touch on creation, embodying the beauty, the mystery, and the tender vulnerability of God.

Maybe, looking longingly on nakedness, is a glorious and practical way to delight in our spouse as well as protect ourselves from lust? When we gaze on sensual curves friends, let us meditate on the deep desires that are bound up in God and allow them to ignite our passion for Him. AW Tozer in his book *Following Hard after God*, says this to us today: "The stiff and wooden quality about our religious lives is a result of our lack of holy desire. Complacency is a deadly foe of all spiritual growth. Acute desire must be present or there will be no manifestation of Christ to His people. He waits to be wanted. Too bad that with many of us He waits so long, so very long in vain." Imagine that.

> *"The stiff and wooden quality about our religious lives is a result of our lack of holy desire. Complacency is a deadly foe of all spiritual growth. Acute desire must be present or there will be no manifestation of Christ to His people. He waits to be wanted. Too bad that with many of us He waits so long, so very long in vain."*

I wonder if all of this tells us that there too is deep desire bound up in God? An infinite wanting even. Yes, a Holy, naked and shamelessly wanton and extravagant desire for you! Even for Him to be able to gaze upon the naked beauty of who you are. God wants you and in all His magnificent beauty invites you to naked oneness with Himself. So, next time you gaze on the glorious nakedness of your beloved, imagine that. God, you see, is not absent form your sex life, but rather is completely bound up in it. This is one way in which the marriage bed is both holy and undefiled. Think about that today. But not too much though, as I'm sure you have work to do!

Listen: *"Whom have I in heaven but You? And there is none upon earth that I desire besides You."* Psalm 73:25

Pray: Lord. I am sorry I do not long to gaze upon You, to be with You. Lord, forgive me. Entice me today O Lord by showing me Your raw, naked and magnificent beauty. Amen.

Night-Whisper | **TRUTH**

Murdering mendacity

A local coffee shop I often frequent when in that area, has an architectural feature that is unique to North America. It has a tin ceiling! Originally, these ceilings were designed as a practical (and cheaper) substitute for elaborately carved and molded plasterwork. Developed in the mid-19th century these mass produced sheets of thin rolled tin plate, became widely available and are today in the USA at least, now emerging back onto the market.

Jeremiah 33:6

Behold, I will bring it health and healing; I will heal them and reveal to them the abundance of peace and truth. NKJV

In Britain, my nation of origin, we only had tin roofs for the outside of houses and there were no tin ceilings. One church which I pastored in the UK met in a very quaint, salmon pink painted tin hut! No honest! It really was.

From my early days, my memory still holds a picture of a ginger tomcat, scampering speedily over the hot tin roof of a garden shed, on a sweltering summer's day in the England of my childhood. Tennessee Williams must have had a similar experience when he wrote his powerful and highly charged moving story of a neurotic, dysfunctional Southern family, with all its rivalries and tensions and avarice. His play, "Cat on A Hot Tin Roof" was produced as a film in 1958 starring, Paul Newman as Brick, Elizabeth Taylor as Maggie and Burl Ives as Big Daddy, the plantation owner and head of the family, whose character by the way, is also terminally ill and knows it.

In one powerful scene, from the bowels of the basement of the large Southern house, where most of the acute action takes place, the father and son, that is, Big Daddy and Brick, emerge after finally facing the truth about one another, who they are and who they have become! They ascend into the light of the sitting room, and Big Daddy turning to Brick, makes this amazing and rabid statement in front of the rest of the family members regarding the disdainful state of affairs as he now experiences it from his new position of clarified truth: "What's that smell in this room?" he shouts. "Didn't you notice it Brick? Didn't you notice a powerful and obnoxious odor of mendacity in this room? There ain't nothin' more powerful than the odor of mendacity. You can smell it. It smells like death."

To be mendacious, is to live a life characterized by falsehood and deception, and yes indeed, it smells like death! Tennessee Williams in "Cat on a Hot Tin Roof" frighteningly reveals the immaturity, constrictions and death that mendacity brings on relationships. The mendacious path we often take is the one that increasingly diverges from the truth of who we are and what we have done to others and ourselves and maybe even, have now become.

> *May I invite you today then, to murder mendacity and to righteously be true to who and all you really are.*

I tell you what friends, no matter how splendid they look, I don't trust tin ceilings and especially not tin roofs! In the wrong way, they cover a multitude of sins and heat up tremendously in the so doing. Any cat will tell you, that tin roofs are far too uncomfortable to sit on.

May I invite you today then, to murder mendacity and to righteously be true to who and all you really are. Take the lid off and look inside! Take the roof off and look up to heaven! Get rid of that powerful and obnoxious odor of mendacity in all the rooms of your house "Cause there ain't nothin' more powerful than the odor of mendacity. You can smell it and it smells like death!" Be true. Be real. Be who you are.

Listen: *"That we should no longer be children, tossed to and fro and carried about with every wind of doctrine, by the trickery of men, in the cunning craftiness of deceitful plotting, but, speaking the truth in love, may grow up in all things into Him who is the head – Christ." Ephesians 4:14*

Pray: Lord. Give me courage to live in the Truth. Give me hope to trust in Your mercy. Give me wisdom, to manage my mouth and Oh my God, help me today, to murder mendacity in me. Amen!

Night-Whisper | **CHANGE**

What Frou-Frou forgot

O ur third cat was most unusual. Marmalade, Piewacket and our last snow white addition, Princess Frou-Frou Tinkerbelle Snowflake or just Frou-Frou for short. Frou-Frou wandered into someone's house on Christmas Eve and somehow arrived with us to be waited on hand and paw from thereon in. She was a most unusual creature.

1 Samuel 17:51

Therefore David ran and stood over the Philistine, took his sword and drew it out of its sheath and killed him, and cut off his head with it. NKJV

I remember one day, for the last time, trying to put her outdoors. I lifted her up and walked towards the door. She was getting agitated at that point so I held her tightly. This freaked Frou-Frou out even more and somehow as I opened the door, she struggled up and out of my grip and sat astride my shoulders. I leaned over to pour her out onto the ground outside. In an instant, she had defied gravitational pull by dropping onto my back and impaling every claw she had all the way through my shirt into my flesh. It was Garfield like in its ridiculousness, for I could not remove the cat from my back without lying on the floor in the house, so she could get off! Whilst lying there and begging her to remove herself, Frou-Frou finally peeled herself off and then ran under the bed. Frou-Frou was a weird cat that enjoyed much more the sterile air-conditioned quiet apartment from the buzzing and warm hunting environment right outside her door. This pampered princess couldn't even kill cicadas on the balcony but insisted on bringing them alive, buzzing in her teeth, as strange gifts to my unappreciative wife and making her responsible for the dispatch!

All our other cats (four more over the years) used us a hotel, coming and a going as they pleased, leaving the odd dead mouse and bird's head as a thank you gift. Sometimes they'd be gone for days. This poor, poor pussy however, was more of a furry slipper than a Jack the ripper kind of a cat. Frou-Frou was the only agoraphobic animal I have ever met! She slept on our bed during the night and anywhere else she found comfortable during the day. Frou-Frou had forgotten the fierce nature that lay within her.

Friends, have you forgotten who you are? Have you forgotten that you are a "stem of that victorious stock" Jesus, Prince of Life; Jesus, Lion of the tribe of Judah; Jesus, Mighty God and Commander of the Armies of the Lord of Hosts; Jesus, King of Kings and Lord of Lords? Have you forgotten who you are? Poor, poor pussy cat, you little diddums you. You are a Lion for goodness sake! So, lift up your voice and ravage, roar against the enemy and rage against the coming of the night. Oh warrior of God! Please remember what Frou-Frou forgot, for I wonder if God is waiting for the heads of all your Goliaths to be placed before His waiting feet? Stop being a pussy!

Poor, poor pussy cat, you little diddums you. You are a Lion for goodness sake! So, lift up your voice and ravage, roar against the enemy and rage against the coming of the night

Listen: *"'Come near, put your feet on the necks of these kings.' And they drew near and put their feet on their necks. 25 Then Joshua said to them, 'Do not be afraid, nor be dismayed; be strong and of good courage, for thus the LORD will do to all your enemies against whom you fight.'" Joshua 10:24-25*

Pray: O Lion King. O mighty God, make me fierce, fearless and bold. Conquering Jesus, forgive me all my Frou-Frou-ness and teach me how to roar today. Amen!

Night-Whisper | **BEWARE**

Samson's soft Sulphur

O f course, it stinks. Sulphur, phew! It smells like bad eggs. Who would want stay anywhere near it and anyway, your inability to breathe correctly around it, surely would force you to run away into some much-needed oxygenated air? However, when it comes to that devilish and secret sniff of sinful Sulphur, many people imbibe on it and seemingly find it very, very attractive. It's true. Our darkness thrives on Sulphur!

Judges 16:20

And she said, "The Philistines are upon you, Samson!" So he awoke from his sleep, and said, "I will go out as before, at other times, and shake myself free!" But he did not know that the LORD had departed from him. NKJV

Sulphur, I have learnt, is deadly but palatable when presented in strange mixes. The beginning of one poem I know reads:

Sulphur Soft
This dawn treads forth
From gilded growling skies
To stroke the wanton curves
And breathe on lover's lies

Ah, unrighteous sex and Sulphur. Be careful now. It's deadly but oh my goodness, it looks and tastes so good.

A wee while ago I was one of those many thousands of people in the area in which I then lived, whilst happily driving along in my car found it coming to a surprising but grinding halt! The fuel gauge still indicated that I was two-thirds full but the attending mechanic told me otherwise. I was empty, bone dry! Thousands of people in the county were experiencing the same issue. Eventually the suppliers of petroleum owned up to the problem. Their refining process had failed to take out the

Sulphur from the mix and too much Sulphur left in the fuel, meant that the electronic float mechanisms in the fuel tanks of many vehicles became inoperative. You were filling up and you thought you were fine but you were in fact deceived. Too much Sulphur in the mix my friends, just too much Sulphur in the mix. Interestingly, not every car exhibited the same problem. Some seemed to cope with the stronger mix, exhibiting no real outward problems. Well, not yet anyway.

Samson's Sulphur was a soft and delicate, desirable and delicious Delilah! It poisoned him slowly and even without him knowing it! So much so, that he went out to do business as usual, thinking he had a full and fully functioning tank, but he came up empty. In the end though, Samson's soft Sulphur left him blind, bound and beaten. Me thinks we are maybe surrounded by many a weeping Samson today? Let me ask you friend "What Sulphurous concoction are you knowingly imbibing on, secretly sniffing?" Let me put it another way, "What's your poison?" Give it up friend, give it up today, for there is only blindness left at the bottom of that bitter cup. You know what I am talking about, so be careful now, be very careful!

"What's your poison?" Give it up friend, give it up today, for there is only blindness left at the bottom of that bitter cup. You know what I am talking about, so be careful now, be very careful!

Listen: *"For Satan himself transforms himself into an angel of light."* 2 Corinthians 11:14

Pray: Lord, give me a nose and a taste for Sulphur today. Lord let me be disgusted; Lord make me vomit; Lord help me run. Amen and amen!

Night-Whisper | **REMEMBER**

Operation over Lord

It's about this time of year that many of us still make sure to remember the D Day Landings in France and indeed, the "Longest Day" needs to be remembered. It is a great danger for our nations to forget.

1 Sam 30:17-19

Then David attacked them from twilight until the evening of the next day. Not a man of them escaped, except four hundred young men who rode on camels and fled. So David recovered all that the Amalekites had carried away, and David rescued his two wives. And nothing of theirs was lacking, either small or great, sons or daughters, spoil or anything which they had taken from them; David recovered all. NKJV

The code name for the extreme left beach of the five chosen for the Normandy invasions was "Sword Beach". Occupying a five-mile stretch of the French coastline it lay 9 miles north of the Hub city of Caen, indeed, all major roads in this sector ran through Caen. It was a key city both to the Allies and their enemy, both for transportation and maneuver purposes.

Ken Oakley was the seaman chosen to act as a bodyguard to the beach master (the most senior person on the beach). His role was to protect him at all times and at all costs. Some of the wounded that lay screaming around him on that day had to be ignored as he carried out his duties towards the beach master. However, Mr.. Oakley does record helping one man who was downed by enemy fire: "I saw Sid." Ken recalls, "He had taken a shell across the back. I put his kidneys back in and put a dressing on. He survived and is still around today (60 years on, 2004) and I was best man at his wedding." Incredible!

I wonder who amongst the angels was the beach master at Bethlehem when God Himself landed on our poor, enemy infested and beleaguered shores? Michael maybe and if so, who among the angels I wonder was His bodyguard? Oh yes, the birth at Bethlehem was a military operation, for such an invasion into enemy territory must not have occurred without some serious angelic battles. I wonder then, if that's why shepherds saw a multitude of the heavenly host? Were they praising God in celebration of yet another battle won? After all, "The Eagle had landed!" The Gospel had arrived! Imagine what talk goes on now I wonder amongst the angels about the day King Jesus, Lord over all, stepped out upon our bloody shores and marched headlong toward Jerusalem and hard faced into enemy territory when just like the lesser David, our King Jesus faced the fiercest foe, conquered him and bought back all!

Imagine what talk goes on now I wonder amongst the angels about the day King Jesus, Lord over all, stepped out upon our bloody shores and marched headlong toward Jerusalem and hard faced into enemy territory when just like the lesser David, our King Jesus faced the fiercest foe, conquered him and bought back all!

The name of all-encompassing operation of the D Day invasions in Europe, 1944 was "Operation over Lord" and the key city to win on that day was Caen. I wonder if the name of God's invasion was "Operation Lord Over All" and the key city won on that day was Bethlehem?

Like Ken Oakley, will you be at the wedding of the wounded but redeemed? "Operation Lord over all" was after all, a complete and utter success!

All things are soon to be made ready for God's big day and the marriage of the Lamb. Be sure to be there. Be sure.

Listen: *"A certain man gave a great supper and invited many, and sent his servant at supper time to say to those who were invited, 'Come, for all things are now ready.'"* Luke 14:16-18

Pray: Certain Savior, make me ready to come to You. Amen!

Night-Whisper | **JUDGE**

Vergissmeinnicht (forget-me-not)

I was brought up reading the poets of the Great War. Brooke, Sassoon, Graves etc. The sickening sites of mechanized warfare in the 1914-1918 First World War, left no sense of honor, especially in the pen of Wilfred Owen. The poem embodying what Owen calls the old lie of 'dulce et decorum est pro-patria mori,' (It's great and glorious to die for one's country) was written after a gas attack. I am not a pacifist but Owen's poem needs to be read by every warrior and every old man that is part of sending younger men to war.

Romans 5:7

For scarcely for a righteous man will one die; yet perhaps for a good man someone would even dare to die. NKJV

Today in Normandy, 1944, another poet, Keith Douglas was killed in action. In 1940, he wrote the poem, which is the title of the Whisper for today, where he speaks of coming again to an area on the battleground, where previously an enemy had tried to kill him. The unburied corpse had lay in the open for three weeks. The closing stanzas of his work, reads as follows:

Look. Here in the gunpit spoil
the dishonored picture of his girl
who has put: Steffi. Vergissmeinnicht.
in a copybook gothic script.

We see him almost with content,
abased, and seeming to have paid
and mocked at by his own equipment
that's hard and good when he's decayed.

But she would weep to see today
how on his skin the swart flies move;
the dust upon the paper eye
and the burst stomach like a cave.

For here the lover and killer are mingled
who had one body and one heart.
And death who had the soldier singled
has done the lover mortal hurt.

As men in the 21st century seek for their emasculated manhood, their stolen status of warrior and adventurer, we must remember the experiences of old, lest we too become the deceived, in thinking death in battle to be a most glorious one.

> *"is the cause you might sacrifice yourself for a good one, a great one, a right one? Make sure it is, for in battle, there will be blood."*

The character of Williams in Shakespeare's *Henry V*, on the eve of the battle of Agincourt, speaks unknowingly to the hidden king who is secretly and disguised, wandering among his frightened host and remarks to him that:

" if the cause be not good, the King himself hath a heavy reckoning to make when all those legs and arms and heads, chopp'd off in a battle, shall join together at the latter day and cry all 'We died at such a place'- some swearing, some crying for a surgeon, some upon their wives left poor behind them, some upon the debts they owe, some upon their children rawly left. I am afeard there are few die well that die in a battle; for how can they charitably dispose of anything when blood is their argument?"

Friends, death is terrible and in battle, people's lives are never lovingly disposed of. Let me ask you today then, my warrior friend, "is the cause you might sacrifice yourself for a good one, a great one, a right one? Make sure it is, for in battle, there will be blood."

Listen: *"But God demonstrates His own love toward us, in that while we were still sinners, Christ died for us." Romans 5:8-9*

Pray: Jesus. We are the worthy cause you died for. Help us then to find and fight in all Your worthy causes today, and if needs be.....

Night-Whisper | **CAREFUL**

Beware of free lunches

In the business world it is a common saying that, "There is no such thing as a free lunch." Yes sir how true, how true, for the purpose of such free feasting is always four fold: Buying, selling, associating, and information gathering, so yes indeed, there is indeed, no such thing as a free lunch.

1 Kings 13:18,19

He said to him, "I too am a prophet as you are, and an angel spoke to me by the word of the LORD, saying, 'Bring him back with you to your house, that he may eat bread and drink water.'" (He was lying to him.) So he went back with him, and ate bread in his house, and drank water. NKJV

Jeroboam had committed terrible spiritual adultery. In the midst of this great transgression a courageous "man of God" of unknown name to us, was then commissioned by God to deliver a message of coming judgment against the idolatrous alter and therefore against its king and practitioners. The prophet's orders from God are clear and direct. "Go, proclaim, don't eat or drink anything, and don't return by the same route." This man of God fearlessly and famously proclaimed the word of the Lord with signs and wonders following and obeyed to the letter the orders he was given that is, until someone offered him a free lunch.

His invitation to a free lunch was not just offered by anybody mind you but by another prophet, older and more experienced than he. However, this old prophet from Bethel lied to the Judean firebrand and so deceiving him, brought him back to his own house for food and fellowship, associating, socializing and information gathering! Whilst chewing on some vitals, there from the old deceiver's very mouth, the Word of the Lord burst out in condemnation toward the deceived and yet disobedient Judean prophet. Here it is, *"After lunch. God is going to kill you!"*

No, I don't like it either and yes, it makes God appear very unfair. After all, a wicked and a lying old prophet together with his sniveling sycophantic sons all live, whilst the brave Judean warrior prophet, perishes in less than understandable and acceptable circumstances.

Friends know these things for yourself today:

Don't fool around with God or His commission to you.

Don't dawdle with directions, or listen to liars, of which there are many, both young and old, fueled by a multitude of intents and agendas all of which are ultimately self-serving.

Don't dawdle with directions, or listen to liars, of which there are many, both young and old, fueled by a multitude of intents and agendas all of which are ultimately self-serving.

Walk wisely, walk carefully and walk with integrity.

Above all, walk with fear and trembling when carrying out the commission of the Great King.

Listen: *"For it is time for judgment to begin with the family of God; and if it begins with us, what will the outcome be for those who do not obey the Gospel of God? And, "If it is hard for the righteous to be saved, what will become of the unGodly and the sinner?"   So then, those who suffer according to God's will should commit themselves to their faithful Creator and continue to do good." NIV*

Pray: Lord, who is sufficient for these things? Who is holy enough and wise enough to stay close and stay careful, to consistently walk so circumspectly? Mercy come a running! Amen.

Night-Whisper | **FORGIVE**

The burying of our pale poppet corpses

If you do just about any reading of Christian writers from previous centuries, they all seem to make mention of a place of restitution, a place of disentanglement, of deliverance, of righting, and of justice which they call the "Great Assizes".

Psalm 89:14

Righteousness and justice are the foundation of Your throne; mercy and truth go before Your face. NKJV

Formerly in Ye Olde England, these Great Assizes, were periodical sessions of the superior courts held in English counties (States) for the trial of civil and criminal cases. These were enormous events and to those not involved, they were almost festive like occasions. In Lancashire for example, the judges would be met at the County border and escorted into town with a great fanfare of trumpets and following lawyers all dressed in their wigs, and whilst their gowns were billowing in the breeze, people in frenzied excitement would run about like headless chickens. (Eat your heart out Judge Judy!)

In essence, these Assizes were places and times that justice was done and was also, seen to be done. The writers of old therefore often referred to The Great Assizes as when God would at last show everything for what it is and justify, reward, or embarrass that which shall indeed, be brought before such a great throne of justice. There are many things that will have to wait until the Great Assizes. Indeed, all things will. Selah!

There is however friends a big problem here, when people, rather than dealing with issues, decide to wait for the Great Assizes. Pastorally I see this problem pictured chiefly, in the continual embracing of death by the hurt, wronged and bitter members of the church.

Let me explain. I have seen people dress their still born child and take their little corpse finger prints and footprints, then coddle, caress hold and photograph the pale poppet of a corpse, before laying them in the grave. Years after though, the pictures of the dead child's corpse can still be found on the mantelpiece and nestled on the sideboard amongst photographs of the living. Others may forget but these so very hurt and dispossessed of parents, will never forget, yes, they will never forget their so great a loss. Do you see what I mean?

What dead child, what pale poppet of a corpse do you hold to your bosom until the Great Assizes? Is it stinking yet?.

Let me ask you today then, what have you lost, or had taken from you that you seek justice for? What has been done to you, said about you, that you believe is wrong? What dead child, what pale poppet of a corpse do you hold to your bosom until the Great Assizes? Is it stinking yet? Look at your sideboard, do you see it there today, that little coffin on the countertop?

It has been my observation that people hold on to hurts, both great and small, when justice does not seem to have been done. People cosset these weeping sores and hold those dead children to themselves because they feel that if they are healed, if that pail poppet of a corpse is finally laid to rest, that they and their unjust hurt, they and their imputed pain will be forgotten and never truly dealt with, never justly dealt with. This kind of fear is not a bad thing, for you see, the true honoring of self, does require the application of justice and we know that such justice may only come at the Great Assizes and lest the Great Judge forget, and frankly we think He just might, then we hold on to our death, we continue to parade its macabre memory in our living areas, so that when we appear before him, He will smell it! He will see it and remember it! You see the cadaverous problem here don't you my dear friends?

There is something deadly debilitating and incessantly insane about such much-loved hurt, such much-loved pain. It really needs to be healed and in the healing it must be buried, and therefore in the beginning and in the end, it must be let go of. Let it be so, for the Righteous Judge will not forget. His throne is one of justice. So, today, O crippled and smelly friend, you must put away the pictures and all the remembrances of seeming injustice and debilitating, unanswered pain. You must begin to live again. Methinks then, that the best of cures for these terrible maladies is that we begin to seek more of mercy than of justice for ourselves and that we also do the same for those others, even for those perpetrators of our hurts.

Let us then dear friends, show mercy today towards ourselves, towards our families, towards those who have hurt us and especially towards those who seek forgiveness from us. If we are big enough, as we get healed enough, then maybe let us go and seek mercy, even towards those hard or ignorant, unrepentant perpetrators of our many painful hurts.

Forgiveness is good ground in which to bury our dead and mercy is a great balm to pour into our still smelly, sore and open wounds.

Listen:

Once there was a broken heart
Way too human from the start
And all the years left it torn apart
Hopeless and afraid

Walls I never meant to build
Left this prisoner unfulfilled
Freedom called but even still
It seemed so far away

I was bound by the chains
From the wages of my sin
Just when I felt like giving in
Mercy came running
Like a prisoner set free
Past all my failures to the point of my need
When the sin that I carried
Was all I could see
And when I could not reach mercy
Mercy came running to me

(Mercy Came Running - Phillips, Craig & Dean (Trust))

Pray: Be merciful to me, O God, be merciful to me! For my soul trusts in You; and in the shadow of Your wings I will make my refuge, until these calamities have passed by. Psalm 57:1

Night-Whisper | **HOPE**

Piercing the paradox

"This absent-minded, overgrown Elf of a man, who laughed at his own jokes and amused children at birthday parties by catching buns in his mouth, this was the man who wrote a book called *The Everlasting Man,* which led a young atheist named CS Lewis to become a Christian." So writes Dale Ahlquist of the American Chesterton society, regarding the great GK himself.

Philippians 2:12b, 13

Work out your own salvation with fear and trembling; for it is God who works in you both to will and to do for His good pleasure. NKJV

You will have to admit that God's servants come in most unusual packages. Whether a con artist like Jacob or a king, like David, God takes their life stories and seems to bend them to His very own design. Well, it really seems like that doesn't it? I wonder though if it simply might appear to be the case, purely from our own miniscule perspective that is? For it seems to me that God's perspective is almost always uniquely, quite, quite different from ours.

As we enter onto this miry ground of the Sovereignty of God and the responsibility of man, let me point to you that there is a danger in this most misunderstood mystery, in this astounding and awesome truth. Maybe even Chesterton can help us here in steering us away from the falling rocks of our own mount minuscule when he highlights the problem to us saying that, "The commonest kind of trouble is that it is nearly reasonable, but not quite." Did you get that? Friends, on this paradoxical playing field of the Sovereignty of God and the free will of man, beware! For here lie the roots of all misunderstandings which eventually grow into trees of heresy. Here as well, lay also the roots of all self-justification that grow into a tsunami of overwhelming sin. So be careful now, careful in the mud and mire of this most troublesome of paradoxes! Careful in using the "nearly reasonable but not quite" justification for the fulfilling of your selfishness, your little godlikeness if gobby proud reflections. Stop blaming the outcome of your choices on the sovereign will of God!

You see, that con man Jacob was in fact authored by God! Yet it as Jacob himself who was, never the less, completely responsible for every scheme he ever initiated, and yet God did not bend His designs or timescales to accommodate even one of the wriggling's of this twister. God did not alter His plan concerning the man, yet nevertheless, the man was responsible for each and every decision! Again, Saul the King, even Saul *as* King, was authored and chosen by God, yet at his sin and disobedience, God then chose David over him instead. Where do the Sovereignty of God and the responsibility of man touch and taste and maybe even turn towards one another? Many have their theories in answer to this question, but while we leave that one for the thoughtful theologians to continue arguing over, today, we still have to try and simply live and live right well mind you, in the light of this great paradox.

When you are powerless, the Sovereign God is still all mighty. When you, the prodigal, when you have been profligate and pitiful even then, the Fathers arms still await you open wide, decked with prepared newness and renewed blessing.

So why not right now begin to pierce this great paradox and let its bursting waters wash you into a better freedom. Yes! Today, obey God, fight for truth, claim the land, trust and believe, hope and endure, for the unfolding of eternity is bound up in the decisions of your faith, or the failures of your sin. Walk carefully here. Walk powerfully here then dear friends. Walk for Him.

Yes, today pierce this great paradox and let its bursting waters wash you into a better freedom, for when you are faithless the Sovereign God is still faithful. When you are powerless, the Sovereign God is still all mighty. When you, the prodigal, when you have been profligate and pitiful even then, the Fathers arms still await you open wide, decked with prepared newness and renewed blessing. When even the locusts have consumed your youthful years, God can make a single day become as fruit bearing as a thousand in His most miraculous renewal. Yes, the only way out of the mud of the Sovereignty of God and the free will of man is to daily lay hard hold of the gracious goodness of our God! Trust in Him.

In the Scriptures, our Father presents us with a great mystery, a perpetual paradox. He is Sovereign and we are responsible. We are corrupt but He is good! Walk in this, in fright, in fight, and in comforting fearlessness, for friends, we shall in the end, find that He works all things well, for He indeed, in astoundingly accurate actuality, works all things well.

Until that day, when we are in heaven and clothed with clarity at last, let us daily pierce the paradox, by laying hold of His great goodness, for it is our only hope of victory.

Listen: *"What then shall we say to these things? If God is for us, who can be against us?" Romans 8:31-32*

Pray: Blessed are you O Lord our God maker of heaven and earth and Upholder of all things. I bow my knee to You today and serve You with reverent fear, smiling in the cheer that Your goodness and Your greatness brings to me. Amen.

Night-Whisper | **CONSIDER**

Fiddling with ferrets

I love shopping for unnecessary plastic objects. If it's a bargain, if it's cheap, then I want it! I mean, who knows when you're going to need five, yes that's right, five red plastic cookie cutters for just $1.99! So you can imagine how much I enjoy shopping at the 50p shops, or the dollar stores. Out of all these treasure houses packed to the gunnels with discount items, Big Lots is my present favorite, as they are particularly great for a speedy throughput of clearance crud. "Get it whiles it hot!" That's what I say!

Galatians 2:10

They desired only that we should remember the poor, the very thing which I also was eager to do. NKJV

So while looking for some cheap cat food I was especially pleased, to come across the final bottle of ear cleaner for ferrets. Yes sir, there it was, a shimmering undiscovered diamond amongst all the other plastic crud! If you want to keep your ferrets aural canal clean before grooming and in between its regular bathing, then this is what you needed, a bottle of ear cleaner for ferrets. After all friends, when was the last time you bathed your ferret? No, come on then, be honest.

Later that most extraordinary day of discovery, I was in the more upmarket discount stores called Target, shopping for cat food again, (yes, the excitement of my Saturdays are sometimes overwhelming as you can imagine!) when I became strangely concerned. Now don't get me wrong here in what I am about to say, for as a family we love the companionship of animals so feeding them is a pleasure for us. However, it was whilst browsing the six aisles dedicated to the care and cosseting of our cats, that I started to get a little uneasy. Six aisles, for goodness sake! One whole aisle at Target, was given over to animal toys, speaking, light flashing, noisy feathery, rubbery chewy animal toys of every description. None of them where cheap either. (Except the small bird toy for cats, that "cheap-ed" when it was pressed or was impaled by claws and teeth.) The other five aisles at Target that day were full of pet food and pet medication! So that was six, massive aisles, all dedicated to the comfort and happiness of our pets. America is truly an amazing place!

At the turn of this twenty first century, Pam Sigler, Co-liaison of USDA Community Food Security Initiative, said that the U.S.A. State of Kentucky alone had 658,000 people living in poverty and 24.9% of those living in poverty were children under the age of 18 and as many as 59,000 Kentucky children were going to bed hungry each night. On top of that, Africa and famine are doing the dance of death upon our silver screens again, again and again, and now, the whole world is moving into a food shortage situation. Nevertheless, I suspect in comparison to humans, that there are very few pets in Kentucky, in America, in Britain, that go to bed hungry each night?

Now, you will forgive me if this is comparing apples and oranges, but isn't there something for us here? After all, at the beginning of the 21st century on our planet, 18,000 children under the age of five died of hunger yesterday. My God! 18,000 children!

God bless you all who practice true religion and long may your example shame the rest of us ferret fiddlers, us consumer Christians into stomach feeding, lifesaving action.

Ferrets are no doubt fun and fascinating and sticking one down your pants must be a real thrill but maybe, just maybe, that bottle of ear-wash, was in fact siphoned from that large lake of hogwash that our Western society and Western churches keep topped up each day by saying, "We have so much material resources because we are Christians and so God has blessed us, but they, the poor that is, especially the Third World poor, have so little because they are not Christians and God has not blessed them." What hogwash! I tell you this brother, until the poor are catered for, the Kingdom of God has not fully come. Not even in Kentucky.

God bless you all who practice true religion and long may your example shame the rest of us ferret fiddlers, us consumer Christians into stomach feeding, lifesaving action.

Listen: *"Pure and undefiled religion before God and the Father is this: to visit orphans and widows in their trouble, and to keep oneself unspotted from the world." James 1:27*

Pray: Father God, Jehovah Jireh, Great provider, give us this day our daily bread and then help us share it with others, in Jesus name we pray, Amen.

Night-Whisper | **EXPECTATION**

Warnings and wellness

You will forgive my often-stated premise that "All poems of true love are in the end, applicable to Jesus." To this end then, let me now quote the opening and closing stanzas from the Victorian poet, Matthew Arnold, and his poem entitled, "Longing":

Job 33:15, 16

In a dream, in a vision of the night, when deep sleep falls upon men, while slumbering on their beds, then He opens the ears of men, and seals their instruction. NKJV

Come to me in my dreams, and then
By day I shall be well again!
For then the night will more than pay
The hopeless longing of the day.

If you are fortunate to sleep say seven hours a day and live for 70 years, then 178,360 hours will be spent asleep. That's 7,432 days, 1,061 weeks, or just over 20 years! If you are overcome with panic at this point, don't go rushing to set your alarm clock earlier, for sleep is important for a multitude of physical, intellectual and psychological reasons. It's also important for spiritual reasons! I wonder then sometimes, if sleep is the only way that God gets time alone with some of us, and gets His opportunity to speak to us?

Of course, I'm talking about dreams. I know, I know, that dreams can be brought on by worry, or the subconscious working of the mind, or environment, or medication and sometimes even food and drink, however, God also speaks in dreams, and maybe more often than we care to acknowledge. The Scriptures and excellent spiritual guidance from other saints, are the key to rightly guiding people in the interpreting and understanding of these things. Through the Holy Spirit and prayer we have the goods to do just this. It is one of my intentions, to at some point turn up at a psychic new age fair and open up my own stall, inviting people to come and have their dreams interpreted. It's not new, indeed, I heard another famous Christian Dr. some years ago report at a conference, that he knew of Christians doing just that, even finding that God had gone before them in terms of prophetic evangelism and had already been speaking to people in their dreams and so had set up the way for them to speak about Jesus! Interesting eh?

Methinks that in dreams, God is interested in communication and especially in two primary forms of communication, those being: warnings and wellness.

It is evident that in the quiet of the night God often, when He has our fullest attention, warns of impending disaster and routes of escape. In addition to this, the Holy Spirit pursues His work of sanctification and under the blanket of sleep, raises problems of both the past and the present, bringing them to the surface of our muddled minds, either defusing the unexploded bombs, or cleaning up the mess of those that have already gone off and devastated our being. Now tell me,

> *It is evident that in the quiet of the night God often, when He has our fullest attention, warns of impending disaster and routes of escape..*

what were you dreaming about last night? Are you keeping a dream journal?

Maybe Arnold's poem, can become our nightly prayer?

> ***Come to me in my dreams, and then***
> ***By day I shall be well again!***
> ***For then the night will more than pay***
> ***The hopeless longing of the day.***

Listen: *"And Pharaoh said to Joseph, 'I have had a dream, and there is no one who can interpret it. But I have heard it said of you that you can understand a dream, to interpret it.' So Joseph answered Pharaoh, saying, 'It is not in me; God will give Pharaoh an answer of peace.'"*

Pray: Jesus, please be my dream maker, Holy Spirit my dream catcher and Great Father, my dream interpreter. Come to me in my dreams, and then, by day I shall be well again! For then the night will more than pay the hopeless longing of the day. Amen!

Night-Whisper | **LIVE**

Tweety birds or twitchers?

One morning a bird landed on our balcony and squawked provocatively at our cat. The cat's lips and whiskers twitched in natural and menacing response. At the right time, she would pounce and nothing would stop her.

Job 41:11-14

"If you lay your hands upon him, you will long remember the battle that ensues and you will never try it again! No, it's useless to try to capture him. It is frightening even to think about it! No one dares to stir him up, let alone try to conquer him. And if no one can stand before him, who can stand before me? I owe no one anything. Everything under the heaven is mine." TLB

"If I do not do, then how can I be?"

I am of course a man of my generation, of my hemisphere, country, and culture and everything that has flowed into these four things for centuries. For example, I have an overwhelming drive from a deep-seated protestant work ethic. I have a very ingrained view of work. Indeed, I feel as a man, that I must work. Like it or not, I find purpose, status, and significance in doing my job. Not that I want to *be* the job but somehow without the job, any job, something inside me, ceases to be, I get sick and slowly die. Strange but true.

"If I do not do, then how can I be?"

Over the years on this planet, my journey has taken me to many places and many jobs. My hardest times have been in periods of "unemployment". Kind and Bible believing Christians have often quoted the verse ***"If a man shall not work he shall not eat"*** to me at those perilous times, for indeed that is what time it is, to a man without a job. Perilous! Maybe we should rather pity the unemployed Christian man and earnestly pray for him? Especially if he's in fellowship with some of those presently employed Bible believers!!

"If I do not do, then how can I be?"

However, over the years I have also observed that there is a greater peril than not having a job and that is, working in a job you hate, simply to put food on a plate, mate. Unfortunately, I have been and have had the misfortune to rub shoulders with thousands of people like this, these "dead men walking," all dutifully pounding the streets of their daily grind and dying in the process; inwardly with rapacious regret. *If a man shall not work he shall not eat* has become a mockery to millions of busy, fat western men, starving inside, dutifully doing something they do not want to do. Somewhere along the way, they have lost their wild ways and the wild Jesus that went with them and church and Christianity for many of them, has become but a dutiful and boring bondage. Maybe this is one reason that less and less men are frequenting our churches, after all, "where's the beef" and of course…

> *Unfortunately, I have been and have had the misfortune to rub shoulders with thousands of people like this, these "dead men walking," all dutifully pounding the streets of their daily grind and dying in the process; inwardly with rapacious regret.*

"If I do not do, then how can I be?"

It is not enough to be, you must also do what you were created to be! Friend, I pray today you will start twitching again, that you will begin to do what you were created to be and that in the so doing, you shall be satisfied with your prey. He who has ears to hear, let him hear.

One morning a bird landed on our balcony and squawked provocatively at our cat. Her lips and whiskers twitched in natural and menacing response. At the right time, she would pounce. Nothing would stop her.

Listen: *"I will not conceal his limbs, His mighty power, or his graceful proportions." Job 41:12*

Pray: Jesus, let me be found faithful but fearless; wild like ocean's rocks, yet steady, steadfast, sure and as beautiful as You created me to be, I ask in Jesus name, O Lord my God. Amen!

Night-Whisper | **DIGNITY**

Designed for dignity

Glasgow band Deacon Blue, brought out an amazing song some years ago now, called "Dignity." I wish I had the space to write out the whole of the lyrics but I haven't, so, I encourage you to go and find them on the web! However, the last few lines of the song "Dignity" read:

Acts 19:15

And the evil spirit answered and said, "Jesus I know, and Paul I know; but who are you?" NKJV

And I'm thinking about home
And I'm thinking about faith
And I'm thinking about work
And I'm thinking about how good it would be
To be here some day
On a ship called Dignity

Dignity. More men need to grapple with this very subject. More of the people of God need to set sail on their own ship of personal Dignity.

Arthur Miller in his marvelous play, *The Crucible* (based on the Salem Massachusetts witch trials of 1692) so wonderfully presents us with the dilemma of the sinful but honest puritan, John Proctor. After wrongly confessing to his participation in witchcraft, he like Latimer of old, later takes back his false confession that would have saved his life, tears it up and cries out "How may I live without my name? I have given you my soul; leave me my name." In desperation the character Hale tells Proctor that he shall hang for not confessing to the sin of witchcraft and even though they all know it was a bogus confession, he should nevertheless, confess! Hale says in effect, "How can you indulge in sinful pride, how can you exchange your life for your name?" The writer Miller, at this point then has the character of Proctor in the crucible of his interrogation, discover the long lost gold of his personal dignity when he replies to Hale saying, "I can. And there's your first marvel, that I can. You have made your magic now, for now I do think I see some shred of goodness in John Procter. Not enough to weave a banner with, but white enough to keep it from such dogs." Proctor then strides aboard his own ship of Dignity, regarding his own personal integrity more than his public reputation. This stand allows Proctor the redeeming of his own character just as much as his true confession, then allows God to redeem his own lost soul.

Truth and honor, Proctor's rediscovered dress of dignity, became more important to Proctor than life itself. As John Proctor goes to his death, his wife Elizabeth weeps in acknowledgement of his rediscovery of his own lost gold, saying: "He has his goodness now. God forbid I take it away." Yes, there is something shining, there is something good, there is something most valuable in personal dignity!

You will never be a man without personal dignity and you will never be a beautiful woman without adorning yourself with the same.

Many of us need to dig deep for this gold of personal dignity, long lost and hanging somewhere in the discarded and dark wardrobe depths of our personal being. You will never be a man without personal dignity and you will never be a beautiful woman without adorning yourself with the same.

Christian friend, what is your name today? What value has heaven and hell set by its exultation or its fall. Consider this today: Who are you? What fragrant scent follows the saying of your name? What value is it both to you and to others? Tell me, what shape is the sail of your dignity when it is unfolded upon the lips of others by the uttering of your lovely name?

Listen: *"Because of the fragrance of your good ointments, Your name is ointment poured forth; therefore the virgins love you." Song of Solomon 1:3 NKJV*

"The syllables of your name murmur like a meadow brook. No wonder everyone loves to say your name!" Song of Solomon 1:3 (from THE MESSAGE):

"A good name is better than precious ointment." Ecclesiastes 7:1

Pray: Lord! Let courage, strength, honor and dignity mark the people You name O God; Lord today, show me more of who I am supposed to be, show me how You see me in the depths of Your heart. Jesus please, help me clothe myself in the dignity and truth, of understanding of who I truly am in You. Amen and amen!

Night-Whisper | **PERSEVERE**

Swing away

Some of you will forgive me I hope if I begin legalistically today, for the Battle of Bunker Hill was legally of course, the British fighting the British and in that sense, we the British won the day! Now let us be even more specific, in saying that in 1775, the British from Britain also won the field today in 1775! (I apologize to my American friends for this most sobering of truths) So, why then is the routing of rebellious British Americans and such a defeat sustained by them, so remembered and so positively celebrated in America today?

2 Sam 23:9b, 10

And after him was Eleazar the son of Dodo, the Ahohite, one of the three mighty men with David when they defied the Philistines who were gathered there for battle, and the men of Israel had retreated. He arose and attacked the Philistines until his hand was weary, and his hand stuck to the sword. The LORD brought about a great victory that day; and the people returned after him only to plunder. NKJV

Well remember that after the British victory that day at Bunker Hill, one half of the regular British forces had been casualties, while only one third of the defending and smaller "rebel militia" had been killed wounded or captured. The attacking British had sustained remarkable losses. I find Bernard Bailyn's conclusions regarding the battle to be most helpful: "It proved that raw, untrained American troops could fight, and fight well - but only if they had to; that success would come to the British only if they responded flexibly and imaginatively to the unorthodox demands of warfare in colonial territories three thousand miles from home; and finally, that if the still disunited, still legally British states of America were to fight with any hope of success, a continental war against the greatest military power on earth, a leader of great personal force and of great military and political skill would have to be forthcoming." And the rest as they say, is history, and so is that rising general, George Washington.

It took three assaults by the regular British forces to secure Breeds hill from the militia, (where the battle was actually fought by the way, not Bunker Hill folks!) and this was chiefly because to preserve ammunition, the militia's General Prescott, had ordered them not to fire until and I quote, "they could see the whites of their eyes." This had a devastating effect on the advancing scarlet-coated lines. There is probably no doubt, that if ammunition had not run out, Breeds Hill would never have been taken! My question today for our consideration is, "Is there a sign in this historic battle for us to learn?" I think so.

It has been said that in writing, the only difference between being an amateur and a professional, is perseverance. In life, often the only difference between defeat and victory is also perseverance.

In the movie starring Mel Gibson called *Signs,* his dying wife, prophetically passes on a message to the brother of Gibson's character, Merrill Hess. Hess, this former slugger baseball player receives the message, which when put into practice at just the right time, defeats the enemy and saves the day. The message for Hess was quite simple, it was just this, "Tell Merrill to swing away."

It has been said that in writing, the only difference between being an amateur and a professional, is perseverance. In life, often the only difference between defeat and victory is also perseverance. So my message to you today dear friend is also so very simple: " Make sure you have enough ammunition, then wait until you see the whites of their eyes, and then swing away dear friends, just keep persevering in swinging away."

Listen: *"And let us not grow weary while doing good, for in due season we shall reap if we do not lose heart." Galatians 6:9-10*

Pray: Lord, help me to persevere in resistance, recovery, redemption and doing what is right. In Jesus name I pray, Amen.

Night-Whisper | **PATIENCE**

Falayta

Having spent many years providing excellent customer service (well I thought so!) I get particularly annoyed when I don't receive it. I must say that nowadays, with the thorough implementation of those most inhuman button pressing or voice activated telephone systems, "service" is a million times worse for the customer.

1Timothy 6:6,7

Now Godliness with contentment is great gain. For we brought nothing into this world, and it is certain we can carry nothing out. NKJV

"Please type in your 27 digit ID number.
Press 1 if you want to rage;
Press 2 if you want to throw stones at the managing director;
Press 3 if you'd like to let his tyres down;
Press 4 if you…"

Well you get the picture.

Then when you finally get through to a human being, it's obvious that it's just some spotty young bloke who still thinks he's speaking to one of his mates and his attitude and lack of people skills, indicate he's probably only just come into puberty! You may want to speak to a manager but this is the best it's going to get! So it's, "Speak to me," the pimply prepubescent from Padooka or "Yeah, whadooyuowan" from me, the embittered dominatrix from Alabama, or "Goodness gracious me, how can I be helping you today," from the part-time belly dancer in Bangalore! Yes sir, customer service has gone global in its pathetic performance!

Oh yes, customer service has gone international and we are invisibly catered for by good folks from a different culture, country, socio-economic planet and time zone! Oh but don't worry, "they will contact you within three billing cycles" if you're lucky. Customer service? Bah humbug! It's outrageous and what's worse is that we, the badly served customers, can do nothing about it!

Now my rising blood pressure over these incidents sometimes get cooled with the outward acknowledgement that though it is awful service, it is never the less out of my control and I can do nothing about it. So, it's profitable for me to examine my trading self and ask why I get so frustrated? I mean, why do I allow myself such a terrible response to such terrible but uncontrollable service? The bad service is out of my control but my response to said bad service, is totally in my control. Do you see what I mean?

"You can't always get what you want, right now! But, If you prepare, plan, save and sow, if you learn the rule of reaping, whilst examining anthills, then maybe patience would become your friend, prudence your pedagogue and success will become your reward?

My conclusion to my personal examination is that my wanting to eat my headphones is partly my need for excellent customer service not being met but mostly, it's because I am part of the "now generation". You see, I want an answer, a solution, a replacement and I want it now!

Columnist Craig Wilson in *USA Today*, speaks of knowing that "quintessential old lady from the depression era, who hoarded all the 'sweet and low' that she harvested from every restaurant she went into. It was the same old lady who at the end of every meal out, would pour the remaining bread rolls into her handbag. They were for later. Maybe for tomorrow's breakfast or for lunch or even for dinner. It didn't matter when they were eaten you know because after all they were 'falayta rolls'." There was no waste, there was no rush. Ahh prudence and patience.

Once I lived next door to an old Polish man that had spent years in a Nazi concentration camp. His back yard was full to overflowing with what everyone, bar him, considered rubbish. Indeed, that's where he got it all from. His daily trip to the rubbish dump! Previous and unimaginable desperate want, had led him to value rubbish. So much so, that he couldn't see anything wasted. I mean anything! He was like the old ladies with the falayta rolls who perpetually and patiently planned for the future because they remembered the want of the past. In our consumer, "Gi'me and gi'me now" society there is a lesson here for us in these old and sometimes injured folk. Maybe even some wisdom?

Here is the lesson: "You can't always get what you want, right now! But, If you prepare, plan, save and sow, if you learn the rule of reaping, whilst examining anthills, then maybe patience would become your friend, prudence your pedagogue and success will become your reward? Patience! It's worth trying and it sure beats getting ulcers!"

Listen: *"Let your conduct be without covetousness; be content with such things as you have. For He Himself has said, 'I will never leave you nor forsake you.'" Hebrews 13:5*

"Go to the ant , you sluggard! Consider her ways and be wise, which, having no captain, overseer or ruler, provides her supplies in the summer, and gathers her food in the harvest. How long will you slumber, O sluggard? When will you rise from your sleep? A little sleep, a little slumber, a little folding of the hands to sleep - so shall your poverty come on you like a prowler, and your need like an armed man." Prov 6:6-11 NKJV

Pray: Naked I came into this world, and naked I shall leave it. All that is necessary for my life and service for You O Lord, You have abundantly provided. In light of these things O my God, teach me then, extravagant sensibleness, dogged preparation and quiet and patient expectancy. In Jesus name I pray, amen!

Jam tomorrow

Whilst having coffee with a friend who managed his own portfolio, I was fascinated to find out the vital need for attentive care, the spreading of risk and the daily monitoring of rise and falls in the market. One of his comments really struck me though when he remarked, "Investments have a fixed and certain return, but all of this stock market 'stuff' is speculation, there's nothing certain about it at all." He's right of course.

Matthew 6:19,20

"Do not lay up for yourselves treasures on earth, where moth and rust destroy and where thieves break in and steal; but lay up for yourselves treasures in heaven, where neither moth nor rust destroys and where thieves do not break in and steal." NKJV

Thomas Friedman (foreign affairs correspondent for the *New York Times*) in his amazing book on Globalization *The Lexus and the Olive Tree* makes the same point consistently. When what happens in Taiwanese markets can the next day disastrously affect jobs in the USA this speculative and interconnected market becomes a serious taskmaster to be either mastered or bowed down to afresh, each and every day! Speculation is like that, go to any gamblers anonymous meeting and ask them. Nothing is certain in the speculative world. Absolutely nothing!

Many years ago as a young Christian in the Royal Navy I was always defending charges that "Christianity has no relevance in the real world, it's all 'jam tomorrow', it's just 'a crutch' for sick people." My answer to Christ being a crutch was simple, "Jesus is more than a crutch for me, He is a wheelchair! I can have nothing without Him. Absolutely nothing!" It's still true today of course.

To answer this charge of "Jam tomorrow," you know, "Pie in the sky by and by," I could and would point to a multitude of historic and present precedents in the miraculously changed lives and directions of peoples and even nations who have turned to Christ. Today however, rather than getting into verbal conflict, I just let it lie. "Pie in the sky?" I reply, "Jam tomorrow? You bet yah baby! For all we see now is passing away and therefore everything to some extent is but a temporary impostor on the eternal stage and yes indeed then, concerning much of Christianity; it is most certainly and most absolutely, jam tomorrow!"

I am increasingly becoming futuristic in my outlook. By faith, I have ceased to speculate but rather, for the first time maybe, I am investing in futures.

I am increasingly becoming futuristic in my outlook. By faith, I have ceased to speculate but rather, for the first time maybe, I am investing in futures. How about you today dear friend? How about you? Do you fancy some jam tomorrow?

Listen: *"For where your treasure is, there your heart will be also."* *Matthew 6:21*

Pray: "Dust and air" O Lord, just "Dust and air" and be it all ever so wonderful, it is passing away, just passing away. My Lord Jesus teach me today the true worth of Your heaven, the value of Your treasure and the timeless nature of Your reward. Keep me from trinkets I pray today. Amen.

Night-Whisper | **WITNESS**

Escaping black holes

My father would often come into my bedroom and cry, "Clean this mess up! It's like the black hole of Calcutta in here!" When I joined the Royal Navy, mess deck inspection by senior NCOs would often be met with the same cry. "Clean this mess up! It's like the black hole of Calcutta in here!" I have of course removed the very colorful prefix that NCOs would often add to such commanding observations! Whatever the black hole of Calcutta was, it was not very nice, well below standards and completely unacceptable.

Jeremiah 38:6

So they took Jeremiah and cast him into the dungeon of Malchiah the king's son, which was in the court of the prison, and they let Jeremiah down with ropes. And in the dungeon there was no water, but mire. So Jeremiah sank in the mire. NKJV

Whether myth or embellished fact, "On 1756, the headquarters of the East India Company was attacked by the anti-British forces of Suraj-ud-Daula, the nawab of Bengal. For but one evening, 146 prisoners were squeezed into the tiny one-room military jail at Fort William. The room measured 18 ft. by 18 ft. so, the room temperature became very high and only a small amount of water was given to just a few prisoners. Consequently, many prisoners died and many others who became too weak to stand were crushed by the other swooning prisoners. In the morning only 23 prisoners were still alive. The jail became known as The Black Hole Of Calcutta".

Even though your Father may have sent you to Dothan, look around Joseph. Where are you now? In a brotherless pit? Look around Jeremiah, Susan, Harry, Zeb, are you in a pit as well? Look around and if you can honestly say that, "It's like the black hole of Calcutta in here," then you've got problems! You've tried to get out no doubt but kept on slipping right back in. Face it friend, you cannot get out of this pit by yourself.

The good news is, that God is in the business of delivering people from black holes. I would venture to say that only He who is the light, has the power to pull us from the desperate gravitational pulls of such soul sucking places.

The threefold solution is simple.

1) Shout

2) Wait and

3) Take any help you can get!

> *The good news is, that God is in the business of delivering people from black holes.*

Shout to the Lord to come and save you, to come and get you out of where you are. Wait and look up. I say again wait and look up! For help is coming. In Jeremiah's case, others were working on his behalf to get him out, even though he knew nothing about it! Eventually, his friends made a rope of old clothes and instructed him to put them under his armpits that they might lift him out. He took what help he could get.

So, if you are in a black and lonely brother-less pit today, just keep shouting friends and look up. Help is on the way, I have no doubt about it!

Listen: *"He also brought me up out of a horrible pit, out of the miry clay, and set my feet upon a rock, and established my steps.*

"He has put a new song in my mouth - praise to our God; many will see it and fear, and will trust in the LORD." Psalm 40:2-3

Pray: This pit is a present one. Primroses or prisons may yet await me. Nevertheless O Lord my God, make me a living book, a powerful proclamation to that great truth, which is the LORD saves! Amen!

Night-Whisper | **PATIENCE**

Quiver time

It was around 1:30am and a good 40-mile drive home in the dark. Driving down those country roads meant it took some time to get there but the fact is I really don't remember the journey home!

2 King 13:17

And he said, "Open the east window"; and he opened it. Then Elisha said, "Shoot"; and he shot. And he said, "The arrow of the LORD's deliverance and the arrow of deliverance from Syria; for you must strike the Syrians at Aphek till you have destroyed them." NKJV

When I boxed, (badly) I had always been able to punch above my weight and was always able to take a good punch as well, ask my doctor! I can still remember the time I awoke out of anesthetic after having my very deviated and dislocated septum put back for the second time. The surgeon was leaning over me, peering into my eyes, his big veined bulbous nose making him look like Rudolph the red nose reindeer and with the remnants of the anesthesia giving his voice a booming and distant quality he said; "Well, what a bloody mess that was!"

He'd fixed my snout up lovely again but he was certainly not impressed that I could take a punch.

In the last round of that particular fight at the Butlins Holiday Park in Bognor Regis, and as usual, my lack of fitness was showing and as the final seconds ticked away my coach got worried that the referee might step in and stop the bout. It had been a grueling one and my opponent certainly was a big hitter. I remember lying back on the ropes as he piled into me, just blocking, covering up, leaning back, shaking my head and laughing at him. His home crowd hated my open disdain of their boy and booed loudly at my shenanigans. It was around midnight, the air was heavy with stale alcohol and blue cigarette smoke but even with the booing, it was obvious that the crowd loved it. I didn't feel a thing. I could take a punch. However, I don't remember the drive home!

With literally less than 20 seconds to go of the last round, my coach threw in the towel and it was all over. I went back to my corner, a bit bewildered at what my coach had done (maybe a bit thankful as well) and he put his arm around by neck and said, "Well done Rob, well done. We've got our own show in two weeks and I just can't risk losing you for that." You see if you get stopped in a fight, it goes on your boxing card and you are not allowed to participate in competition for three weeks. The club's own annual show is usually its only real major money making event for the year and so it needs its boxers fit, ready, and approved for competition. If that means throwing in the towel now, so be it. A more important battle lies ahead.

Some of you have been taken off the pitch and are surprised at your recall. Some of you are itching to get back into the fray. Steady now, steady. The great coach knows what He is doing.

Some of you are on the bench looking on at what is happening on the field. Some of you have been taken off the pitch and are surprised at your recall. Some of you are itching to get back into the fray. Steady now, steady. The great coach knows what He is doing. He purposes a victory for the whole team, not just you. Friend, when the time is right, He shall reach back into His quiver and find your feathers ready for flight and in an instant you shall feel the tension of His mighty bow, drawing back, drawing back, back, back until the release of His sure like grip, shall send you swiftly to the center of His chosen target. Be patient friends, be patient, for God has got His own club's show that He is saving you for!

Listen: *"...In the shadow of His hand He has hidden Me, and made me a polished shaft; In His quiver He has hidden Me." Isaiah 49:2b*

Pray: Lord. Help me to make good use of Your "quiver time". Amen.

Singing kings

"Et Eärello Endorenna utúlien...
Sinome maruvan ar Hildinyar tenn' Ambar-metta!"

So sings King Aaragon in Tolkien's *Lord of the Rings: The Return of the King.* Just in case you cannot speak "Elvish," (hu hu, hu hu, thank you very much momma) King Aaragon is singing. "Out of the Great Sea to Middle-earth I am come. In this place will I abide, and my heirs, unto the ending of the world."

Zephaniah 3:17

"The LORD your God in your midst, The Mighty One, will save; He will rejoice over you with gladness, He will quiet you with His love, He will rejoice over you with singing." NKJV

A multitude of thoughts flow out of Tolkien's great and marvelous trilogy, this lake of pictures filled to the full by Tolkien, but what struck me most during these final scenes, is that after the King is crowned, it is only then that he breaks into song! It really took me back. I can understand Royalty having great choirs singing for them, even picked soloists to serenade them but when the crowned King himself gets up and starts singing, well I can hear the shattering of some boundaries as they fall to the ground in my head.

Imagine now King Jesus. Crowned and surrounded by innumerable beings of light; beings so awesome that current language fails in its descriptive ability! Imagine the noise of the redeemed, each one with a new song in their own hearts. Imagine the cascading clinking of millions of crowns cast before the Lamb on the floor of the crystal sea and then finally, imagine if you will, a silence in heaven, as the Savior slowly stands and lifts up His voice; and moving through the vast throng of angels towards His awaiting bride, He begins to sing.

This song is prepared and practiced from before the beginning of time. It surpasses in description both the depth and the glories of the songs of the angelic sons of God as they once sang together in the morning light of creation, because each word sung in the Saviors song, settles your soul, salves your wounds, searches out the long questions of your heart and answers them in love and tender compassion.

Have you ever imagined friends, a singing Savior? What a wedding singer eh? What a wedding singer indeed.

Friends, our Savior sings! Do you hear Him today, do you really hear Him?

Listen: *"They sing the song of Moses, the servant of God, and the song of the Lamb." Rev 15:3*

Pray: Sing me a lullaby that Your soft and tender peace would wash o'er my troubled soul. Sing me a marching song that I may possess the land. Oh sing me some songs of merry magic, Jesus Lord my Savior and open up to me the unfathomable depths of who You are O Lord. Sing to me Savior, oh sing to me today. Amen and Amen!

Have you ever imagined friends, a singing Savior? What a wedding singer eh? What a wedding singer indeed

Night-Whisper | **REJOICE**

Dancing divinity

It makes me sweat. You know? Public dancing. Something deadly happened to my rhythm a long while ago under a disco ball in a church hall somewhere far away and it's now atrophied. So when it comes to weddings and fun nights that involve dancing… oh dear. Bring on the deodorant.

Luke 15:25

Now his older son was in the field. And as he came and drew near to the house, he heard music and dancing. NKJV

I am always astonished to find films rooted in their locality doing so well globally, an old film called *The Full Monty* being one of them. I giggled watching it again on TV in America for a number of reasons. First, though the film had been censored for the American audience by removing all the expletive "F" bombs, they had left a multitude of even worse words and phrases in the movie! These local curse words obviously were not yet a global commodity! Secondly, I laughed at just how well the film was received and yet how much of the pathos and passion contained therein just had to have been missed by folks from another culture, folks from another world. After all, the American common mind-set is very, very far removed from Yorkshire. I've never been a male stripper but I have stood in those job lines and sat on those benches under miserable skies wondering where I'm going to get work. *The Full Monty* is so true in its portrayal of out of work desperation that it brings back far too many of my own bad and jobless memories and moves me to tears.

In the film, there is one stunning scene in particular that is of interest to us today. The fat male dancer called Dave (he went on to act as lead in a CBC comedy, *Still Standing*) funnily fights against the lie that "fat is a feminist issue," by being thoroughly ashamed of his own plump proportions. He wonderfully portrays the out of work, overweight man who has lost his dignity, his devotion and his sex drive. In the saddest of scenes, Dave tearfully asks his wife "Who would want to see him, a fat guy dancing?" His wife tenderly, lovingly and longingly looks at him and says "Me. I would Dave. Me."

Sin, has robbed many of us of our joy, and turned our dancing into mourning. Pharisaic religion has done the same for far too many more of us. However, the extravagant God has a party going on! There is even now rejoicing in the presence of the angles over one sinner who repents. How else would God rejoice but with laughter, and singing and dancing? I wonder if king David might have asked God one day saying "Who would want to see me a murderer, an adulterer, a deceiver, a liar, a fallen and broken man. Who would want to see me dancing?" And I wonder if God looked tenderly, lovingly and longingly on him and said, "Me Dave. I would. Me."

> *Sin, has robbed many of us of our joy, and turned our dancing into mourning. Pharisaic religion has done the same for far too many more of us.*

Listen: *Lee Ann Womack in her song "Dance," maybe nicely sums up a challenge for the atrophied of soul today friends. "Promise me that you'll give faith a fighting chance. And when you get the choice to sit it out or dance. (slight pause) Dance! I hope you dance."*

Pray: Lord. Truly turn my mourning into dancing before Your gracious triumphant holy and ever rejoicing, oh so happy throne. Amen!

Night-Whisper | **LOVE**

Finding forgiveness

Set in South Carolina in 1964, *The Secret Life of Bees* by Sue Monk Kidd tells of a motherless daughter's discovery of "family". The main character, young Lily Owens, flees town after springing her "colored" friend from jail. Taking residence with a trio of black bee keeping sisters Lily finds the love of a mother she never had. It is revealed that as a young girl, Lily Owens accidentally killed her momma with a gun and this is the secret shadow that has dogged her, her whole young life.

Jeremiah 31:3

The LORD has appeared of old to me, saying: "Yes, I have loved you with an everlasting love; therefore with loving-kindness I have drawn you." NKJV

Sue Monk Kidd, with great insight, presents the scene where Lily finally forms on her lips her crippling confession. As the author puts it, "this was the time and place she spilled out her guts and then hoped she wasn't tossed out to sea to wait for her punishment." A most devilish scene is then presented to us. Lily, weeping before her friendly confessor, during the discarding of all her sins and hurts, then experiences the most wounding accusation of all against her. The writer describes it again and most magnificently so, saying "Probably one or two moments in your whole life you will hear a dark whispering spirit, a voice coming from the center of things. It will have blades for lips and will not stop until it speaks the one secret thing at the heart of it all. Kneeling on the floor unable to stop shuddering I heard it plainly. It said, 'You are unlovable Lilly Owen. Unlovable. Who could love you? Who in this world could ever love you?'" And friends, there we have it. The one secret thing at the heart of it all, for us all. When all is revealed, when the garbage is dumped on the floor for God to pick through and everyone to see, who in this world could ever love us?

Forgiven in Jesus yet still believing this lie becomes a cancerous disability; becomes a menaced muteness, a weight too much for anyone to bear, a lie too horrific for anyone to believe. Yet deep in our heart, we clutch this poisoned thought and our ears bleed shut to God's whispers of love. Cut by the bladed lips of dark and deceiving spirits that come to us in our shame and our confession and many times, often well before and long time after such desperate declarations, our tired and tearful eyes are poked out with sharp sticks of condemnation and so, being blinded to God's love and compassion, we are forced to retreat into our sour and sorry dens of self-protection and continue to live out the lie, that no one in this world, no one, could ever love us.

"City of God. Dearest Jerusalem. Despite your broken walls, your poisoned waters and your dark, dark streets, I know your name. I know where you live. I love you. I think you're wonderful. You are more precious to me than all the named and shining orbs that hang in My sky. I love you I tell you. I just love you!"

The same God that says in our old nature "Dwells no good thing" also says that we are "more precious than the sum of this whole wonderful world and everything in it put together." We don't believe it though! Not really. Our lives are testimony to that.

I wonder if God were to push a little love note under the door of our heart today that it might say: "City of God. Dearest Jerusalem. Despite your broken walls, your poisoned waters and your dark, dark streets, I know your name. I know where you live. I love you. I think you're wonderful. You are more precious to me than all the named and shining orbs that hang in My sky. I love you I tell you. I just love you!" Well, there it is friend, next to the doormat of your heart! Read that note. Believe it. It's true.

Listen: *"The LORD builds up Jerusalem; He gathers together the outcasts of Israel. He heals the broken-hearted and binds up their wounds. He counts the number of the stars; He calls them all by name." Psalm 147:2-4*

Pray: Deliver me from the cruel lips of lying spirits, lying books and lying men oh Lord. Help me to possesss my loveliness before You O God my lovely Savior, O Christ my bleeding sacrifice, O Jesus lover of my scarred and broken soul. Amen.

Night-Whisper | **VICTORY**

Who's your daddy?

You may have heard the old joke of the soldier who instead of receiving a rifle when visiting the quartermaster, is given a stick instead. "It's not a problem," says the quartermaster, "It's a magic stick, just point it at the target and say 'bang' and the enemy will fall." Sure enough, the soldier enters battle with his magic stick and points it the enemy soldiers loudly shouting, "Bang! Bang! Bang!" Astonishingly, with each shout an enemy would fall down dead. All accept one of them that is, who despite not holding a weapon himself, nevertheless continues to walk steadily towards the soldier bearing the magic stick. As the enemy walks by, his hands held out in front of him as though he is clutching an invisible steering column, he is heard repeating constantly, "Tanka, Tanka, Tanka, Tank!"

1 Chronicles 12:22

For at that time they came to David day by day to help him, until it was a great army, like the army of God.
NKJV

Before D Day, to give the impression that the assault was coming from elsewhere, a great deal of time was spent by the allies in positioning wooden tanks and wooden mock up aircraft in their thousands, at points far away from official loading zones, thus deceiving the enemy as to the Allies' true intentions. Indeed, during dire conflict, it has been known for soldiers to even take the exhausts off jeeps and drive them slowly up and down in the darkness, again thus giving the far greater force of the enemy the perception that heavy armor was now maneuvering into position against their forthcoming attack. These tactics of deception are not new for humans, animals or insects! Indeed, the insect world is replete with tricky little decoys to stop the smaller and the weaker, from falling into the hands of the bigger and stronger prey.

Enemy deception against the Christian often acts in reverse and so friends, we have been deceived into thinking that we are the puny ones! I am not calling for blind stupidity in the face of the enemy folks but I am calling for an open heaven and some open eyes for the people of God to see who they truly are and to see what they have truly got! Honestly, the chariots of God are twenty thousand, even thousands of thousands and the Lord is among them. His forces, our forces, are massive and He is the greatest warrior of all!

Today the great King amidst His forces still shouts loudly saying *"As I live forever, If I whet My glittering sword, and My hand takes hold on judgment, I will render vengeance to My enemies, and repay those who hate Me. I will make My arrows drunk with blood, and My sword shall devour flesh, with the blood of the slain and the captives, from the heads of the leaders of the enemy." Deuteronomy 32:40-42.* Now let me ask you today Oh whimpering one, "Who's your Daddy, Christian? Who's your Daddy?"

Now let me ask you today Oh whimpering one, "Who's your Daddy, Christian? Who's your Daddy?"

Unless you want cheese with that whine, I suggest you stop that little pity party the enemy's deceit has caused you to invite all your friends to and begin to see things as they really are, for you, have been deceived!

Listen: *"And Elisha prayed, and said, 'LORD, I pray, open his eyes that he may see.' Then the LORD opened the eyes of the young man, and he saw. And behold, the mountain was full of horses and chariots of fire all around Elisha." 2 Kings 6:17-18*

"You are of God, little children, and have overcome them, because He who is in you is greater than he who is in the world." 1 John 4:4

Pray: Little me, stands in the middle of the Mighty and the Almighty. Let me see it today O Lord. Let me see it today and then let me grow into the warrior You have called me to be.

Night-Whisper | **FORGIVE**

When "Ilunga" is not good enough!

The BBC's Oliver Conway reported on a list of "the hardest words to translate" which was drawn up from a consultation with 1,000 linguists. At the top of the list, from the DR Congo came the word "Ilunga." Ilunga means "a person who is ready to forgive any abuse for the first time, to tolerate it a second time but never a third time." Now friends that may be a hard word to translate but it seems incredibly gracious and realistic to practice. Don't you think?

Matthew 6:12

And forgive us our debts, as we forgive our debtors.
NKJV

Whatever the sin, if I forgive you once, then to myself, and others I can appear to be magnificently magnanimous. It may cost me, it may cost me dearly but I yes I, have forgiven you. I feel better than you when I do this. Yes, that's the right thing to do, yes, that's gracious, yes, that's reasonable. Should you commit a sin against me for a second time, then I can choose to tolerate it. My forgiveness would be less magnanimous, maybe tainted with a not a little annoyance but everyone would understand why. Yes, that's right, yes, that's kind of gracious, yes, that is just about reasonable. Now, sin against me the same sin a third time and I would be a fool to let it go! To let my grace be stomped on, to let my grace toward you be abused, even raped, I would be fool. Three strikes and your out! That's reasonable friends. Yes, that's very reasonable! Don't you think? Of course you do.

The hardest thing to do is to forgive the deliberate and persistent sinner! It's most unreasonable. However, the apostles came to realize that they were not following a reasonable Master. Jesus demanded total obedience, not a reasonable following. Jesus raised the bar far higher than any human could reach by themselves, for Jesus expected His followers in forgiveness, to be like God! To a man, the apostles all baulked at this, for truly, us forgiving others their persistent sins against us, is the hardest thing on earth to do and frankly, it cannot be done, I say again, it cannot be done, without the grace of God o'er flowing our hearts and us trusting totally on Him for help in both the forgiving and the forgetting. You see,

Ilunga just is just not good enough for grace, so you had better get on your knees!

Listen: *"Take heed to yourselves. If your brother sins against you, rebuke him; and if he repents, forgive him. And if he sins against you seven times in a day, and seven times in a day returns to you, saying, 'I repent,' you shall forgive him. And the apostles said to the Lord, 'Increase our faith.'"* Luke 17:3-5

Pray: And when seven seems leap-able, You raise it to seventy O Lord and when that is visible, You raise it to seventy times seventy. How can this be done? Except You give wings to my feet and put heaven and eternity in my eyes and grant an openness to my hard heart and a deep, so very deep, consciousness of all You have forgiven me, I just cannot forgive in the way You want me to. Great God grant it, and increase my faith in doing so, help me never settle for Ilunga, when Ilunga is not good enough. Amen.

The second hardest thing to do

It took a combination of poverty and the pigpen to drive the prodigal home. It took the prophet Nathan and nine months of fear to break the heart and knees of the adulterer and murderer, king David. The passage of time and the death of a loved one always sink their hooks into the prodigals hearts to help drag the buggers back.

Luke 15:18-19

I will arise and go to my father, and will say to him, "Father, I have sinned against heaven and before you, and I am no longer worthy to be called your son. Make me like one of your hired servants." '
NKJV

A poem written in Derbyshire dialect, based on a prodigal hurriedly rushing into the local hospital before his father dies, reads:

Avf cum tu see me fatheh
Is jus cum in todayh
I wint te see im at is aahse
But thid whisked him reet away

Avf cum tu see me fatheh
Cause we avn't spoken much
An I've missed is kindly words
Ave missed is gentle touch

Avf cum tu see me fatheh
Cause I've only got but one
And I yam is bloody prodigal
And I yam 'is loving son

Avf cum tu see me fatheh
Afore he gus away
I've come to tell 'im "sorry dad
I wish that you would stay

I wish I hadn't let thee dahn
I wish I weren't reet freetened

I wish me eyes were cool deep pools
I wish me lips were sweetened"

Avf cum tu see me fatheh
Before it's all too late
To tell 'im that I love him
That I've left the land of hate

Avf cum tu see me fatheh
Ave come to get me ring
I've come to hold his old grey head
And hear his strong heart sing

The first hardest thing may be to forgive the persistent "pig penner" but the second hardest thing to do, is to ask for forgiveness from others. Friends, what will it take? What will it take, to gain the gift of a broken heart that only God can fix? If you want to be whole, if you want to be restored, then you must seek forgiveness from those you have hurt, offended and let down. Do it today.

Listen: *"If we confess our sins, He is faithful and just to forgive us our sins and to cleanse us from all unrighteousness. If we say that we have not sinned, we make Him a liar, and His word is not in us." 1 Jn 1:9-10*

Pray: Have mercy upon me, O God, according to Your loving kindness; according to the multitude of Your tender mercies. Blot out my transgressions. Wash me thoroughly from my iniquity and cleanse me from my sin. Amen and Amen.

Night-Whisper | **FORGIVE**

The right words at the right time

In the United Kingdom it was Ronan Keating of Boyzone that popularized the lyrics of the song "Baby Can I hold You Tonight". In North America, that job was left to Tracy Chapman.

Jeremiah 3:12

Go and proclaim these words toward the north, and say: "Return, backsliding Israel," says the LORD; "I will not cause My anger to fall on you. For I am merciful," says the LORD; "I will not remain angry forever. Only acknowledge your iniquity." NKJV

I truly believe that God is not silent in culture. Maybe the author of the books *Peace Child* and *Lords of the Earth*, Don Richardson, had it right many years ago when he postulated that, "Every culture is bejeweled by relevant images of redemption and we just have to find them." I believe he was correct! Much more, I believe that God speaks today and constantly so, both in culture and through culture. You may have to pan the muddy rivers friends but the good gold of God is shining there! So it is, with the profound lyrics of this song, listen:

Sorry
Is all that you can't say
Years gone by and still
Words don't come easily
Like sorry, like sorry

Forgive me
Is all that you can't say
Years gone by and still
Words don't come easily
Like forgive me, forgive me

I love you
Is all that you can't say
Years gone by and still

Words don't come easily
Like I love you, I love you

But you can say baby
Baby can I hold you tonight
Maybe if I told you the right words
At the right time you'd be mine

This song tells, even re-enforces two things for us today.

First, that true repentance does not come easily. It really is a work of grace that may sometimes, take the years of a lifetime. Sorry, does not come easily.

> *True repentance does not come easily. It really is a work of grace that may sometimes, take the years of a lifetime. Sorry, does not come easily.*

Secondly, that confession, regret and turning can be encapsulated, indeed must be encapsulated at the right time, with the right words of "sorry, forgive me and I love you." When this is done the God who appears to be afar off, will be draw near to us and we shall know that He is ours and we shall know that we are His.

Maybe Dame Elton John was right as well? For all of us, "Sorry seems to be the hardest word!" Nevertheless, let us seek with tenacity and tears, these true places of repentance so that we may say…

Listen: *"I am my beloved's, and my beloved is mine." S.O.S. 6:3*

Pray: For I acknowledge my transgressions, and my sin is always before me. Against You, You only, have I sinned, and done this evil in Your sight - that You may be found just when You speak, and blameless when You judge. Lord, I am so sorry for my sin. Please forgive me.

Night-Whisper | **FORGIVE**

The third hardest thing

Let me conclude this little trilogy on forgiveness with the weeping test. It is a common misconception from those outside Christ to look into the confessional and grieving aspects of the repentant sinner and conclude that Christianity is a miserable path to walk. Indeed, the fact that many of us in the church are strangely and wonderfully happy to remain in the "wormology" that the Biblical presentation of original sin seems to present, simply re-enforces that observation. To the astonished outside I say, "Behold the journeying Christian. What a cup of groaning Joy!" To the dour dark and dismal wormologist brethren groaning under the burdens of their failings I say, "For goodness sake. Stop it! You're giving Jesus a bad name. Be the cup of groaning joy you should be!"

Genesis 50:15-17

When Joseph's brothers saw that their father was dead, they said, "Perhaps Joseph will hate us, and may actually repay us for all the evil which we did to him." So they sent messengers to Joseph, saying, "Before your father died he commanded, saying, 'Thus you shall say to Joseph: I beg you, please forgive the trespass of your brothers and their sin; for they did evil to you.' Now, please, forgive the trespass of the servants of the God of your father." And Joseph wept when they spoke to him. NKJV

The problem here is both simple and profound. It is simply that we have yet to acquiesce and splash around like little children, like kittens, fire-cracking in fighting, rolling and biting, kicking and meowing on the soft carpeted floors of the outrageous all forgiving nature of God. It seems that our cultural Christianity has deemed that we should be more humbly thankful and respectfully quiet regarding our forgiveness, than astonishingly vocal and as happy as a hippy on speed and friends, don't wheel out the old "Aunt Sallys" of the fixed in stone nature of both temperament and culture. We are supposed to be joyful and there is nothing more outrageously joyful than found and felt forgiveness! The problem is, we have failed to possess such forgiveness and the evidence of this is three fold:

First, our miserable hands in the pockets, good grief not this old chorus again, lackadaisical and pathetic excuses for worship celebration services.

Secondly, a distasteful slowness in the forgiveness of others.

Thirdly, a reluctance to forgive ourselves.

This last one is important and no doubt is the cause of the first two problems.

What will He do with you eh? You old misery guts! What will He do with you who are still waiting for the non-existent hammer to fall?

You see, the third hardest thing to do friends is to receive forgiveness. The brothers had already been thoroughly forgiven by Joseph and their concocted story regarding the care of their departed Father was simply an echo of their inability to forgive themselves. They still condemned themselves and feared his retribution. At this, Joseph wept.

Today friends let me ask you this; does Jesus weep for wriggling worms that should be splashing children? What will He do with you eh? You old misery guts! What will He do with you who are still waiting for the non-existent hammer to fall?

Listen: *"'Now therefore, do not be afraid; I will provide for you and your little ones.' And he comforted them and spoke kindly to them." Genesis 50:17*

Pray: Let me hear Your gentle words today say to me "Do not fear, little flock, for it is your Father's good pleasure to give you the kingdom." Amen. Luke 12:32-33

Night-Whisper | **WORK**

'Bout a lazy farmer that wouldn't hoe his corn

Alison Crouch and Union Station preserve their bluegrass roots very well with their rendering of a traditional ballad called "The Young Man Who Wouldn't Hoe Corn". Songs of tradition contain a message and sometimes, even a few! This particular song opens with the words:

Proverbs 24:30

I went by the field of the lazy man, and by the vineyard of the man devoid of understanding; and there it was, all overgrown with thorns; its surface was covered with nettles; its stone wall was broken down. NKJV

Tell You a little story
And it won't take long,
'Bout a lazy farmer
Who wouldn't hoe his corn.
The reason why I never could tell,
That young man was always well.
Come September
There came a big frost
All the young man's corn was lost

In case you didn't know, hoeing corn was in those days, the consuming but necessary business of weeding. The moral is simple, attend to your weeding else you shall not have a crop.

Jesus tells us that hearing the Word is not sufficient for Christians. The soil also needs attending to. Some of us, indeed, most of us in the West, have more weeds in our field than corn! The weeds are easy to identify, listen: *"Now he who received seed among the thorns is he who hears the word, and the cares of this world and the deceitfulness of riches choke the word, and he becomes unfruitful."* (Matthew 13:22-23) Friends, anything that hinders growth is a weed. Pull it!

If you purpose a good crop, then you must hoe your corn. You must take time to weed out cancerous cares and destructive desires. You must take time! Got it? Spirituality takes time and your spiritual life takes effort. Allow me to challenge you practically today. Are you healthy, are you well? Are you producing corn, you know, food! If Not, then you need to get to it friend, get going and get hoeing, else you shall be without a crop. In your life, you can't do without consistent T and E; do you know what I mean, "time and effort."

Listen: *"When I saw it, I considered it well; I looked on it and received instruction: a little sleep, a little slumber, a little folding of the hands to rest; so shall your poverty come like a prowler, and your need like an armed man." Proverbs 24:32-34*

Pray: Lord, so far this proverbial trinity of "little things" has cost me dearly. Help me Lord to hoe my soil diligently, so that I may produce a hundred fold of what You have planted, for You indeed purpose a full crop in my life. Amen!

DID YOU REMEMBER?

DON'T FORGET TO ORDER YOUR NEXT QUARTER OF NIGHT WHISPERS.

Check us out more at WWW.NightWhispers.com

Buy at WWW.WhisperingWord.com

THE MISSION STATEMENT OF THE 66 BOOKS MINISTRY

WWW.66Books.tv | Our Mission is:

1.   "To proclaim Jesus, the Savior of the whole world, from the whole Bible, because He is wonderful!"

2.   Indeed, we are constrained by the love of God, to communicate the rawness of the Bible to real people, in real ways, and our driving and major project of '66Cities' shall take us to the 66 most influential cities of the 250 nations of the world in the next 25 years. That's 16,500 cities!

3.   We are aiming to build relationships with grass roots, real people, that is, ordinary people, who, in their own countries and cities, want to do extraordinary things for Jesus and the Kingdom of God, to bring a Biblical Gospel message that is relevant to now, in a world that has come to believe that Jesus is irrelevant to their lives.

If you would like to partner with us in this great task. Then we want to hear from you! Contact me today on vr@66books.tv

MORE ABOUT 'THE 66 BOOKS MINISTRY'

<u>WWW.66Cities.com</u> | By the year 2047, by the grace of God and according to His will and favor, The 66 Books Ministry shall be preaching consecutively from each of the 66 Books of the Holy Bible, the Gospel of the Lord Jesus Christ in 16,500 of the most influential cities of the world on an annual and ongoing basis!

We do not underestimate the quality teams of trained people that this will take, together with the need for vast amount of materials and finances which will also have to be raised. However, as most futurists indicate that the growing global population will be gathered mostly in major world cities in the coming years, there is a necessity laid upon the church to present and proclaim the God of the whole Bible, through the primacy of preaching in these cities. We are convinced that this is a paramount and pressing concern.

"For since, in the wisdom of God, the world through wisdom did not know God, it pleased God through the foolishness of the message preached to save those who believe" 1 Corinthians 1:21NKJV

233

"Preach the Word! Be ready in season and out of season. Convince, rebuke, exhort, with all longsuffering and teaching." 2 Timothy 4:2NKJV

The church is looking for a revival. The 66 Books Ministry, however, is trying to start a revolution of a return to the preached Word, from the whole of the Bible as a precursor to any and all coming revival.

For "whoever calls on the name of the Lord shall be saved." How then shall they call on Him in whom they have not believed? And how shall they believe in Him of whom they have not heard? And how shall they hear without a preacher? And how shall they preach unless they are sent? As it is written: "How beautiful are the feet of those who preach the gospel of peace, Who bring glad tidings of good things!" Romans 10:13-15 NKJV

We are unashamedly looking for and seeking to foster a massive, huge, releasing, transformative, and exceptionally disruptive reversal and revolutionary change, both within the church and then in the world. We are not just another mission trying to do the same as every other mission. We are intent on revolution!

To this revolutionary end, we have no fear of seeming failure and will cultivate that audacious atmosphere within our ministry. We want to attract grass roots people who are people of faith risk takers, for we believe it is people of such life hazarding attitudes that are used by God to make breakthroughs in the world for the Kingdom of God. Hanging back for fear of seeming failure, hanging back and waiting for the trained professionals, both wastes the time of the church time and kills the spirit of victory.

In that spirit then, we therefore are believing that this task can be accomplished by such people within the time frame we have given ourselves.

Fully assured then, that we are in full obedience with the great commission of our great God and Savior Jesus Christ, we do, with great confidence in Him, turn ourselves happily to this so great a task in the hope that, like a happy hound straining at the leash to be let loose, we believe that many other people will smile along with us and be part of this brand new grass roots 21st Century Global City Mission.

If you want to know more and want to be part of what we are doing then go to www.The66BooksMinistry.com or call us in the USA on **855 662 6657**, or email V.R. directly on vr@66Books.TV

AUTHOR BIO | PURPLE ROBERT

It won't take too much investigation for you to find out that Purple Robert is in fact, Victor Robert Farrell (Born 1960 and alive until now and still kicking) was born in Chesterfield England to Scottish parents with Irish grandparents, which is an obvious recipe both for writing and emotional disaster if ever there was one!

He grew up a culturally excluded Roman Catholic (his parents were divorced,) which is one of the reasons why he hates religion with a passion, and that's an interesting enough fact by itself, because he is also an ordained protestant minister to boot.

Purple Robert. became a Christian whilst serving on board a Polaris Submarine at the end of the cold war. He has gone on to do many things, including being a broadcaster, App developer, performance poet, and the long-time author of 'Night Whispers,' which is read in over 100 counties and is also translated into Spanish (see www.Night Whispers.com)

Currently, Purple Robert is also President of The 66 Books Ministry: a grass roots global city mission endeavor. I suppose it is this concoction of background and experience which means Purple Robert's communication is always raw and emotive. After all, and as he says, *"If Christianity can be relevant on a Monday morning, several hundred feet underneath an unknown ocean, in a pornographic sewer pipe carrying enough nuclear weapons to destroy a continent whilst hiding from the Russians, then it can be relevant anywhere and everywhere!"*

Purple Robert sees himself as a servant of the 'Word of the Lord' to tasked communicate the God of the whole Bible. His proclamation of the same is done in very raw terms to very real people, is both his burden and his passion.

·MORNING· → **|·HISTORICAL·BOOKS¶**

· **BOOK·11·of·66·** → **|·1·KINGS·16,17¶**

Signpost·Words → **|·"AN·ANSWER'¶**

Highlight·Verses → **|·1·Kings·16:31-34¶**

And·it·came·to·pass,·as·though·it·had·been·a·trivial·thing·for·him·to· walk·in·the·sins·of·Jeroboam·the·son·of·Nebat,·that·he·took·as·wife· Jezebel·the·daughter·of·Ethbaal,·king·of·the·Sidonians;·and·he·went· and·served·Baal·and·worshiped·him.·Then·he·set·up·an·altar·for·Baal· in·the·temple·of·Baal,·which·he·had·built·in·Samaria.·And·Ahab·made· a·wooden·image.·Ahab·did·more·to·provoke·the·Lord·God·of·Israel·to· anger·than·all·the·kings·of·Israel·who·were·before·him.·In·his·days· Hiel·of·Bethel·built·Jericho.·He·laid·its·foundation·with·Abiram·his· firstborn,·and·with·his·youngest·son·Segub·he·set·up·its·gates,· according·to·the·word·of·the·Lord,·which·He·had·spoken·through· Joshua·the·son·of·Nun.·NKJV¶

Some·Observations·→·|¶

This·is·nothing·but·an·extended·killing·time,·and·it·is·God·who·is· slaughtering·His·wayward·nation.·Decade·after·decade·the·decadent· mobster·kings·steer·the·people·more·and·more·out·of·the·way·of·the· Lord.·Dogs·lick·up·the·blood·from·slaughtered·corpses,·birds·peck· the·watery·eyeballs·out·of·the·maggot·eaten·heads.·Death·and· destruction·stalk·the·land,·yet·still·the·people·rise·up·to·pray·to·an·idle· and·engage·in·sexual·sin.·The·mercy·of·God·is·seen·on·two·legs·and· heard·from·one·mouth,·even·the·prophets·of·the·Lord.·Now,·dropped· from·heaven,·out·of·nowhere,·in·answer·to·the·madness·of·Ahab·the· loon,·a·prophet·like·no·other·arrives·on·the·scene.·Elijah·the·Tishbite¶

A·Call·To·Action·→·|¶

Fine·pulpits·and·finer·churches,·are·rarely·the·abode·of·the·prophet.¶

·EVENING· → **|·PAULINE·EPISTLES¶**

· **BOOK·46·of·66·** → **|·1·CORINTHIANS·15¶**

Signpost·Words → **|·"ASSURANCE·OF·SALVATION'¶**

Highlight·Verses → **|·1·Corinthians·15:1-11¶**

Moreover,·brethren,·I·declare·to·you·the·gospel·which·I·preached·to· you,·which·also·you·received·and·in·which·you·stand,·by·which·also· you·are·saved,·if·you·hold·fast·that·word·which·I·preached·to·you—· unless·you·believed·in·vain.·For·I·delivered·to·you·first·of·all·that· which·I·also·received:·that·Christ·died·for·our·sins·according·to·the· Scriptures,·and·that·He·was·buried,·and·that·He·rose·again·the·third· day·according·to·the·Scriptures,·and·that·He·was·seen·by·Cephas,· then·by·the·twelve.·After·that·He·was·seen·by·over·five·hundred· brethren·at·once,·of·whom·the·greater·part·remain·to·the·present,·but· some·have·fallen·asleep.·After·that·He·was·seen·by·James,·then·by·all· the·apostles.·Then·last·of·all·He·was·seen·by·me·also,·as·by·one·born· out·of·due·time.··For·I·am·the·least·of·the·apostles,·who·am·not· worthy·to·be·called·an·apostle,·because·I·persecuted·the·church·of· God.·But·by·the·grace·of·God·I·am·what·I·am,·and·His·grace·toward· me·was·not·in·vain;·but·I·labored·more·abundantly·than·they·all,·yet· not·I,·but·the·grace·of·God·which·was·with·me....·NKJV¶

Some·Observations·→·|¶

The·two·'wee'·words·we·Evangelicals·dislike·to·discourse·upon·are· 'if'·and·'unless.'··I·believe·that·once·we·are·saved·we·are·always· saved,·'IF'·we·continue·on·receiving,·believing·and·standing.·I· believe·that·once·we·are·saved·we·are·always·saved,·'UNLESS'·we· prove·ourselves·to·be·unfaithful·and·reprobate·in·forsaking·the·Christ· of·the·Scriptures.·Paul·did·not·believe·he·was·saved·by·our·works,·yet· by·grace·he·worked·his·little·heine·off.·¶

A·Call·To·Action·→·|¶

Continuance·in·the·work·of·grace·is·the·key·to·your·own·assurance.·¶

JOIN THE FELLOWSHIP OF THE BOOK

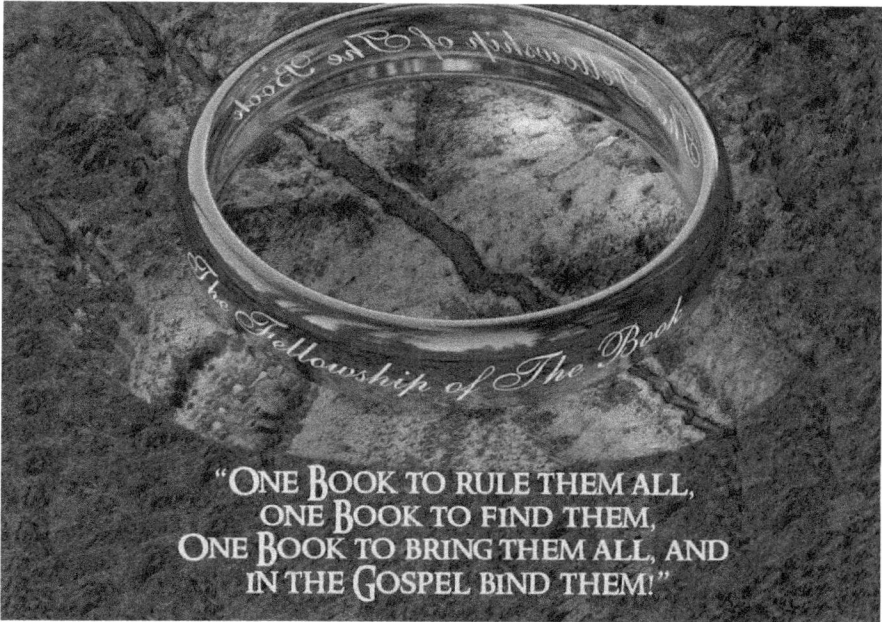

"ONE BOOK TO RULE THEM ALL,
ONE BOOK TO FIND THEM,
ONE BOOK TO BRING THEM ALL, AND
IN THE GOSPEL BIND THEM!"

WWW.TheFellowShipofTheBook.com

The Fellowship of The Book is a Daily Bible Reading Fellowship. It is a morning and evening devotional of four books available each quarter of the year. It includes

Signpost Words
Highlight Verses
Some Observations
Call To Action

Consecutively, Chronologically and in many other ways, Read The Bible Thru in 1 just one year, with both Morning and Evening reading to keep your mind focused on the Lord of the Word and the Word of The Lord. Buy this and several other ways to 'Read the Bible Thru in a Year Books' at www.whisperingword.com

ANOTHER BOOK BY THE AUTHOR, VR

Habakkuk A Prophecy For Our Time

As the Church in the West is found to be mostly dead and covered with Laodicean lukewarm vomit, as The Lord, slips the dead things silently over the side of the storm tossed ship into the dark oblivion of the waves of secular humanism and rising Islam, what remains will need to be fortified with steel to live in a quickly changing anti-Christian world of persecution. There is no better prophecy more equipped to speak to such a remnant who shall be so very besieged. Welcome to Habakkuk, 35 of 66, a prophecy for our time.

Buy at www.whisperingword.com

ANOTHER BOOK BY THE AUTHOR, VR

The 66-Minute Bible

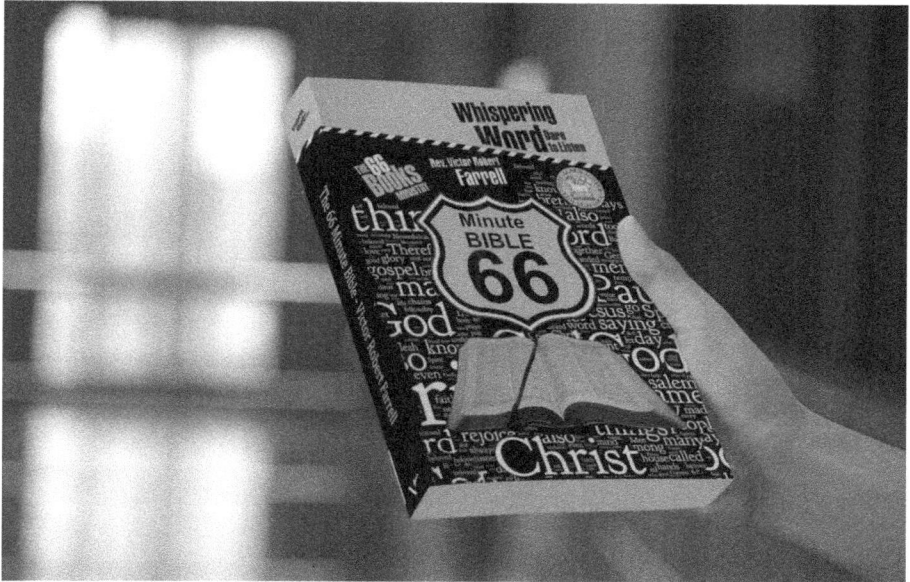

I am told that there are 788,258 words in the King James Bible and of these 14,565 are unique. That's a lot of words! I have been reading the Bible for nearly forty years on an almost daily basis. It still remains to me the most exciting book on the planet, however, it never gets any easier. Bible reading is a spiritual discipline and for me the emphasis is on discipline. I created this resource to aid you in your Bible reading, it gives your brain a sixty second overview of the Bible, a loose enclosure to herd the narrative of the book into something that can be seen as a whole. It was never created to be a substitute, but an aid. Just saying...... Friends, welcome to the most exciting book on the planet! V.R.

Buy at www.whisperingword.com

AN INTRODUCTION TO 'PURPLE ROBERT'

Some Dangerously Different Devotionals!

Now, before I go any further, this guy comes with warning shots! The opening parts of his currently seven volumes pf poetic works says quite clearly, *"If you are easily offended by low level expletives…**Go no further. Do not read this book!** If you are prudish in any way …**Go no further. Do not read this book!** If you do not want to be challenged…**Go no further. Do not read this book!** If you want to be stroked into unchanging sleep and into the stupor of remaining as you are…**Go no further. Do not read this book!** If you hide under the respectable covers of a comfortable religion…**Go no further. Do not read this book!** If you are frail in faith and dishonest about life under this sun…**Go no further**. If you have no real integrity regarding the state of your own heart, **then do not read this book!** If however, you are grown up, honest and have a basic human integrity, ENJOY!"* So, there you go, you have been warned!

Purple Robert is a Performance Poet and a Metaphysical Biblical Realist. If you want to hear some of his work and get hold of the 66 Poems each of the Seven volumes contain, then go to www.PurpleRobert.com and purchase them today.

Also Buy at Buy at www.WhisperingWord.com